FLORIDA TEST PREP

FSA Practice Test Book

English Language Arts

Grade 4

ISBN 978-1974005826

CONTENTS

INTRODUCTION
For Parents, Teachers, and Tutors

About the Florida Standards Assessments (FSA)

Students in Florida are assessed each year by taking the Florida Standards Assessments (FSA). The FSA English Language Arts test covers reading, language, and listening. In Grade 4, the test also includes a writing component where students write either an opinion piece or an informative/explanatory essay. This practice test book will prepare students for this test. It contains three complete practice tests that are similar to the real FSA English Language Arts tests, as well as a writing task for both opinion and informative/explanatory writing.

Types of Tasks on the FSA English Language Arts Test

The FSA English Language Arts test contains four types of tasks. These cover reading, language and editing, listening, and writing.

- Reading - students read a passage and answer questions about it. Around 75% of the test questions cover reading.
- Language and editing - students read a short passage that contains errors and identify how to correct the errors.
- Listening - students listen to a passage and answer questions about it.
- Writing - students read several texts, and then write an opinion piece or essay based on the texts.

This test book contains all four types of tasks. Just like the real test, there is a greater focus on reading. Each practice test in this book ends with two listening tasks. To complete these tasks, students will need to have the passages read to them. The passages are included at the end of the book.

Types of Questions on the FSA English Language Arts Test

The test contains four types of questions. These are multiple choice, multi-select, open response, and hot text.

- Multiple choice - students select the one correct answer from four possible options.
- Multi-select - students select all the correct answers from the possible options.
- Open response - students provide a written answer. Questions may require a short answer of just a few words, a longer answer of one or more paragraphs, or may involve completing a diagram or a web.
- Hot text - students select words, phrases, or sentences to answer a question. Students may be asked to select words or phrases, select sentences in a passage that support an answer, or place items in order.

This test book contains all four types of questions. By completing the practice tests, students will become familiar with all the question types they will encounter on the real FSA English Language Arts test.

Taking the Test

Each practice test in this book contains 78 or 79 questions. This is longer than the actual FSA test, which has from 56 to 60 questions. The additional length ensures that all skills are tested and a wide range of question types are included. Each practice test is divided into two sessions. Students can complete the two sessions on the same day or on different days, but should have a break between sessions. Each session should be completed in 90 minutes. The writing tasks are similar to those found on the real tests. On the actual test, students will write either an opinion piece or an informative/explanatory essay. This book contains one practice set for each type of task. Each writing task should be completed in 2 hours.

Florida Standards Assessment

English Language Arts

Practice Test 1

Session 1

Instructions

Read each passage and answer the questions that follow it.

For each multiple-choice question, fill in the circle for the correct answer. For other types of questions, follow the instructions given. Some of the questions require a written answer. Write your answer on the lines provided.

Grooming a King Charles Cavalier

The King Charles Cavalier is a small breed of Spaniel dog. It is known as a toy dog by kennel clubs. They are very popular in the United States and around the world. These dogs have a silky coat and can be difficult to groom. Professional groomers can carry out the task. However, many owners choose to save money and groom their dog themselves. It takes some patience, but you can learn to groom a King Charles Cavalier.

Start by making sure you have the correct equipment to groom your dog correctly. You will need:
- a comb
- a brush
- dog-friendly conditioner

 You should complete these steps when your dog is clean. If your dog's coat is dirty, give the dog a bath first. Then dry the coat before starting.

Step 1
Before you start, make sure that your dog is in a comfortable position either on your lap or on a blanket. Your dog should be nice and relaxed.

Step 2
Take your comb and move it smoothly through the coat. There may be some knots or tangles, so be sure not to comb it too fast. You don't want to pull at the dog's fur, cause your dog any discomfort, or scare it. Be gentle, but make sure that all dead or matted hair is removed.

Step 3
Once the combing is complete, add some of the conditioner to the coat. This will add shine and make it easier to brush your dog.

Step 4
Comb your dog's coat for a second time to make sure that it is as smooth as it can be.

Step 5

It is now time to brush your King Charles Cavalier. Hold the brush firmly in your hand and be sure to keep your dog still. Move the brush gently through your dog's coat. Take care to smooth out any lumps or patches of uneven hair. Move through each area of the coat twice.

Step 6

Once you've finished brushing, condition your dogs coat again. This helps to keep your dog's coat free from tangles. It will also make it easier to groom your dog in the future.

Step 7

Lastly, all you need to do is gently pat the dog's coat dry. Your dog is now nicely groomed and the coat should stay that way for around 4 to 6 weeks.

You can give your dog a small food reward after you've finished the grooming. This will help make sure your dog looks forward to being groomed.

1   Read this sentence from the passage.

> **Be gentle and make sure that all dead or matted hair is removed.**

Which word means the opposite of <u>gentle</u>?

Ⓐ   Calm

Ⓑ   Fast

Ⓒ   Rough

Ⓓ   Slow

2   In the sentence below, what does the word <u>silky</u> mainly describe?

> **These dogs have a silky coat and can be difficult to groom.**

Ⓐ   How long the coat is

Ⓑ   How the coat feels

Ⓒ   What the coat smells like

Ⓓ   What color the coat is

3   Circle **all** the steps that the conditioner is used.

Step 1   Step 2   Step 3   Step 4

Step 5   Step 6   Step 7

4   Describe **two** reasons it is important to comb the dog's coat slowly and carefully.

1: _____

_____

2: _____

_____

5   Select **all** the benefits of using conditioner. Tick the box for each benefit mentioned in the passage.

☐   To add shine to the coat

☐   To stop the coat from getting tangles

☐   To prevent the dog from getting fleas

☐   To remove dirt from the dog's coat

☐   To make it easier to brush the dog

☐   To help the dog relax

6 What is the main purpose of the passage?

   Ⓐ   To teach readers how to do something

   Ⓑ   To entertain readers with a story

   Ⓒ   To inform readers about a type of dog

   Ⓓ   To compare different types of dog products

7 What is the purpose of the bullet points?

   Ⓐ   To describe the steps

   Ⓑ   To give useful hints

   Ⓒ   To list the items needed

   Ⓓ   To highlight the key points

8 The first tip says to complete the steps when the dog is clean. Why do you think it is important that the dog is clean? In your answer, describe **two** problems you might have if the dog's coat is dirty.

_____

_____

_____

_____

_____

_____

9   Which detail from the photograph is most relevant to the passage?

    Ⓐ   The size of the dog

    Ⓑ   The color of the dog

    Ⓒ   The look of the dog's fur

    Ⓓ   The look on the dog's face

10   According to the passage, what should you do right after brushing the dog?

    Ⓐ   Comb the dog's coat a second time

    Ⓑ   Condition the dog's coat

    Ⓒ   Rinse the dog's coat

    Ⓓ   Give the dog a treat

11   Complete the web below by listing **three** reasons to support the idea that it takes patience to groom a King Charles Cavalier.

It takes patience to groom a King Charles Cavalier.

12 If you owned a King Charles Cavalier, would you groom it yourself or pay a professional to do it? Explain why you made that decision.

_____

_____

_____

_____

_____

_____

_____

_____

_____

_____

_____

_____

_____

_____

Keep Smiling

Happiness is something special,
To be enjoyed by young and old,
And then be shared by one another,
To keep us warm through winter's cold.

Whatever time or season,
Or hour of the day,
Happiness can lift your spirits,
More than words could ever say.

And turn your sadness into joy,
Make a smile from a frown.
It brings a burst of gentle laughter,
And lifts you up when you are down.

Without it life is nothing,
Just a pale shade of gray.
An everlasting stretch of nighttime,
That waits patiently for day.

So make the most of living,
And make happiness your friend.
Greet it warmly and keep smiling,
Keep happiness close until your end.

And never doubt its power,
To bring enjoyment out of sorrow,
And leave you smiling through your slumber,
As you wait to greet tomorrow.

13 What does the word <u>sorrow</u> most likely mean in the line below?

To bring enjoyment out of sorrow,

Ⓐ   Boredom

Ⓑ   Problems

Ⓒ   Sadness

Ⓓ   Peace

14 What does the line below mean?

Happiness can lift your spirits,

Ⓐ   Happiness can be hard to find.

Ⓑ   Happiness can make you feel better.

Ⓒ   Happiness can feel like floating.

Ⓓ   Happiness can bring people closer.

15 Based on your answer to Question 14, choose **two** lines that have about the same meaning. Write the **two** lines you have chosen below.

Line 1:

_____

Line 2:

_____

16 The poet describes how life can be "just a pale shade of gray" to show that life can be –

Ⓐ simple

Ⓑ weird

Ⓒ boring

Ⓓ difficult

17 Read this line from the poem.

It brings a burst of gentle laughter,

Which literary technique does the poet use to help the reader imagine sudden laughter?

Ⓐ Alliteration

Ⓑ Simile

Ⓒ Metaphor

Ⓓ Flashback

18 What is the rhyme pattern of each stanza of the poem?

Ⓐ All the lines rhyme with each other.

Ⓑ There are two pairs of rhyming lines.

Ⓒ The second and fourth lines rhyme.

Ⓓ None of the lines rhyme.

19 What type of poem is "Keep Smiling"?

Ⓐ Rhyming

Ⓑ Free verse

Ⓒ Limerick

Ⓓ Sonnet

20 Which statement best describes the theme of the poem?

Ⓐ You should have fun while you are young.

Ⓑ Every day is a chance to try something new.

Ⓒ It is important to be happy and enjoy life.

Ⓓ There is no time like the present.

21 Hyperbole is the use of exaggeration to make a point. Which line from the poem contains hyperbole?

Ⓐ *To be enjoyed by young and old,*

Ⓑ *Make a smile from a frown.*

Ⓒ *An everlasting stretch of nighttime,*

Ⓓ *As you wait to greet tomorrow.*

22 The poet states that happiness can "keep us warm through winter's cold." Explain what the poet means by this.

_____

_____

_____

_____

_____

23 The poet chose a field of flowers as the background photograph for the poem. Why do you think the poet chose this photograph? In your answer, explain how it relates to the theme or the tone of the poem.

_____

_____

_____

_____

_____

24 Describe what the poem teaches you about happiness and sadness. In your answer, give **three** reasons it is important to keep smiling.

_____

_____

_____

_____

_____

_____

_____

_____

_____

_____

_____

_____

_____

_____

Baseball

Baseball is a bat and ball sport that is very popular in America. It is a game played between two teams of nine players. The aim of the game is to score runs. Players strike the ball with a bat. Then they run around four bases. When they cross home base again, they have scored a run. Home base is also known as the home plate. The bases are set at each corner of a 90-foot square called the diamond.

Each team takes it in turns to bat while the other fields. The other team must stop the batters from scoring runs by getting them out. To get a batter out, they can strike them out. This means that the batter misses the ball three times. They can also get them out by catching the ball if the batter isn't safe on a base. Players can stop at any of the four bases once they have hit the ball, which makes them safe.

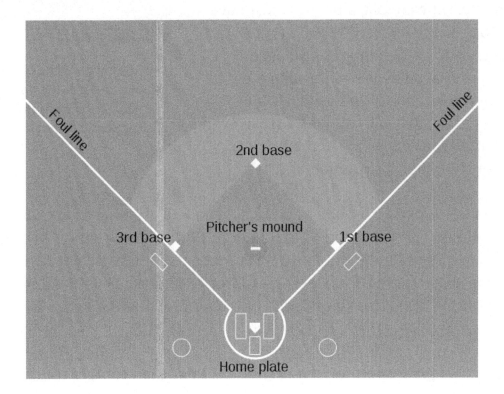

Once three players are out, the fielding team takes their turn to bat. Each time a team bats, it is known as an innings. There are nine innings in a professional league game. The team that scores the most runs at the close of all innings is the winner. The player who throws the ball to the batting team is known as the pitcher. Each professional game has at least two umpires who ensure fair play between the teams. Some big games have six umpires. There is one at each base and another two along the foul lines. The umpires know that their decisions could change the game, so they watch their areas closely.

The umpires judge whether players on the batting team are out or not. This usually means working out whether the player touched the base before the fielder touched the base with the ball. Umpires also decide whether or not pitchers throw the ball correctly. For example, a pitcher must have one foot on the pitcher's mound at the start of every pitch. The umpires also judge whether each pitch passes through the batter's strike zone. If the ball does pass through, the pitch will count as a strike even if the batter does not swing. If the ball is too high or too wide, it is counted as a ball.

The umpire watches closely. If the runner reaches the base before the fielder receives the ball, he will be safe and will not be out.

Baseball developed from the traditional bat and ball games of the 18th century. It has a sister sport referred to as rounders. Both of these sports were first played in America by British and Irish immigrants. It has since developed to become known as the national sport of North America. Over the last 20 years, the sport has also grown worldwide. It is now very popular in the Caribbean, South America, and many parts of Asia.

Baseball is a great sport for young kids. It is safer than contact sports like football. It requires a range of skills. Players can focus on being good batters, pitchers, or fielders. At the same time, players learn to work together as a team.

25   Read this sentence from the passage.

> **Each professional game has at least two umpires who ensure fair play between the teams.**

Which meaning of the word <u>fair</u> is used in this sentence?

     Ⓐ   Average

     Ⓑ   Just or correct

     Ⓒ   Pale

     Ⓓ   Sunny or clear

26   What is the player who throws the ball to the batting team called?

     Ⓐ   Bowler

     Ⓑ   Runner

     Ⓒ   Catcher

     Ⓓ   Pitcher

27   Which sentence from the passage is an opinion?

     Ⓐ   *It is a game played between two teams of nine players.*

     Ⓑ   *Each time a team bats, it is known as an innings.*

     Ⓒ   *Over the last 20 years, the sport has also grown worldwide.*

     Ⓓ   *It is safer than contact sports like football.*

28   What does the diagram most help the reader understand?

Ⓐ   How many players are on a team

Ⓑ   The main rules of baseball

Ⓒ   Where the bases are located

Ⓓ   What the purpose of the pitcher is

29   Circle **all** the terms related to baseball that are explained in the passage.

platform   goal   home plate

diamond   coach   innings

tackle   net   strike zone

30   Choose **two** of the words you circled in Question 29. Write a definition of each word below.

Word: _____

Meaning: _____

_____

Word: _____

Meaning: _____

_____

31 The passage was probably written mainly to –

    Ⓐ   encourage people to play sport

    Ⓑ   teach readers about the sport of baseball

    Ⓒ   show why baseball is popular

    Ⓓ   describe the history of baseball

32 Read this sentence from the passage.

    Players strike the ball with a bat.

Which word could best be used in place of strike?

    Ⓐ   Swap

    Ⓑ   Shove

    Ⓒ   Hit

    Ⓓ   Throw

33 Complete the web below by listing **three** things the umpires judge.

The Role of the Umpires

34 What is the main purpose of the information in paragraph 5? Describe how the purpose is different from the main purpose of the passage overall.

_____

_____

_____

_____

_____

35 How does the photograph help explain why an umpire is placed at each base in big games? Use details from the passage to support your answer.

_____

_____

_____

_____

_____

36 The author says that baseball is a "great sport for young kids." Do you agree with this? Use details from the passage to explain why or why not.

_____

_____

_____

_____

_____

_____

_____

_____

_____

_____

_____

_____

_____

The passage below contains errors. The words or phrases that are incorrect are underlined. For each word or phrase underlined, answer the question below.

The Great Barrier Reef

The Great Barrier Reef is found off the coast of Queensland in Australia. It is the <u>most large</u> reef in the world. The reef is protected. This will help it stay healthy for many years. It is important that the reef is not lost. It is too unique and <u>speshal</u> to be lost. It really must be saved, <u>and</u> that all people can enjoy it.

A lot of people travel to the reef each year to see the coral and fish. There are many beautiful and interesting fish to be <u>saw</u>. It is quite an <u>amazeing</u> sight. It has been said that the reef is <u>won</u> of the seven natural wonders of the world.

37 Which of these should replace <u>most large</u>?

   Ⓐ   larger

   Ⓑ   largest

   Ⓒ   most larger

   Ⓓ   most largest

38 Which of these should replace <u>speshal</u>?

   Ⓐ   special

   Ⓑ   speshial

   Ⓒ   spechial

   Ⓓ   spesial

39   Which of these should replace <u>and</u>?

    Ⓐ   but

    Ⓑ   for

    Ⓒ   so

    Ⓓ   yet

40   Which of these should replace <u>saw</u>?

    Ⓐ   see

    Ⓑ   seen

    Ⓒ   sees

    Ⓓ   seeing

41   Which of these should replace <u>amazeing</u>?

    Ⓐ   amazing

    Ⓑ   amazzing

    Ⓒ   amazzeing

    Ⓓ   ammazeing

42   As it is used in the sentence, what is the correct spelling of <u>won</u>? Write your answer below.

_____

END OF SESSION 1

Florida Standards Assessment

English Language Arts

Practice Test 1

Session 2

Instructions

Read each passage and answer the questions that follow it.

For each multiple-choice question, fill in the circle for the correct answer. For other types of questions, follow the instructions given. Some of the questions require a written answer. Write your answer on the lines provided.

Muhammad Ali

 Muhammad Ali is a famous American boxer. He was born in 1942. Many people believe that he is the greatest boxer of all time. Ali won the World Heavyweight Championship three times. He fought on four different continents. He had his first success as an amateur boxer. In 1960, he won an Olympic gold medal. During this time, he was known as Cassius Clay. He changed his name in 1964.

Ali became known as a fast and powerful fighter. He was also very confident. He often predicted which round he would win each fight. Some people thought he should be more humble, while others loved his attitude. He won his first title in 1964 after beating the fearsome Sonny Liston. Ali defended his title several times. By 1967, he was considered to be unbeatable. Then the Vietnam War occurred. Ali was meant to go to war, but he refused. He was unfairly stripped of his title. He was arrested and had his boxing license taken away. He fought the charges. He won his right to freedom. He also won the right to box again. In 1971, he continued his career.

He had lost some of his speed and power. However, he still reclaimed his title twice. He had famous bouts with Joe Frazier and George Foreman. He won both of these fights. His last fight was against Trevor Berbick in 1981. He was not as quick as usual, and he lost the fight.

He retired with a career record of 56 wins and 5 defeats. Ali now spends much of his time working with charities. In 1996, the Olympics were held in Atlanta. Ali was chosen to light the torch. It was a great way to honor a great sportsman.

His honors have not only been given to him for his sporting achievements. In 1999, he was awarded the Presidential Medal of Freedom. This is the highest medal an American civilian can receive. He was awarded the medal not only because of his sporting successes, but for his service to others and his efforts in promoting peace and equality. When awarding him the medal, President George W. Bush described Ali as "a fierce fighter and a man of peace." This is a good way to sum up Ali's achievements.

43   Read this sentence from the passage.

Ali became known as a fast and powerful fighter.

Which word means about the same as <u>powerful</u>?

Ⓐ   Angry

Ⓑ   Quick

Ⓒ   Skilled

Ⓓ   Strong

44   Choose the word that completes the definition of the word <u>reclaimed</u>. Write the word on the blank line.

after   more   less   again   before

claimed _____

45   Who did Ali defeat to win his first boxing title?

Ⓐ   Sonny Liston

Ⓑ   Joe Frazier

Ⓒ   George Foreman

Ⓓ   Trevor Berbick

46   The passage is most like –

Ⓐ   a biography

Ⓑ   an advertisement

Ⓒ   an autobiography

Ⓓ   a news article

47   Which detail from the passage is least important to the main idea?

Ⓐ   Ali is thought of as the greatest boxer of all time.

Ⓑ   Ali fought on four different continents.

Ⓒ   Ali won his first world title in 1964.

Ⓓ   Ali had 56 wins and 5 defeats.

48   Select **all** the sentences below that contain opinions.

☐   *In 1960, he won an Olympic gold medal.*

☐   *During this time, he was known as Cassius Clay.*

☐   *He was unfairly stripped of his title.*

☐   *Some people thought he should be more humble, while others loved his attitude.*

☐   *His last fight was against Trevor Berbick in 1981.*

☐   *It was a great way to honor a great sportsman.*

49   Which sentence from the passage best supports the idea that Ali was a successful boxer?

Ⓐ   *Ali won the World Heavyweight Championship three times.*

Ⓑ   *During this time, he was known as Cassius Clay.*

Ⓒ   *He often predicted which round he would win each fight.*

Ⓓ   *Ali now spends much of his time working with charities.*

50   How is the passage mainly organized?

Ⓐ   A problem is described and then a solution is given.

Ⓑ   Events are described in the order they occurred.

Ⓒ   Facts are given to support an argument.

Ⓓ   A question is asked and then answered.

51   Complete the web below by listing **three** actions that were taken against Ali when he refused to take part in the Vietnam War.

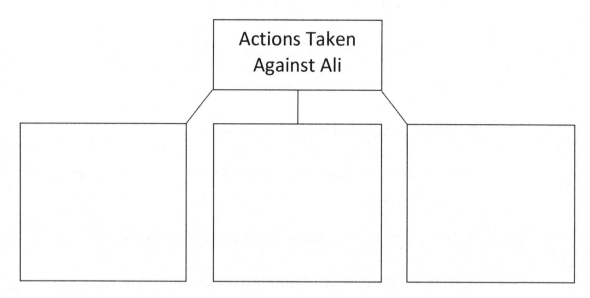

Haunted House

Marvin refused to believe in ghosts. Even on Halloween, he would not get scared when his friends Steven and Jason shared horror stories. They would gather in his bedroom and sit in pale lamplight talking about ghosts and goblins. The scary stories only made Marvin laugh.

One night they were at Marvin's house enjoying a sleepover. His friends decided to test how scared of ghosts Marvin really was.

"After he has fallen asleep, let's play a trick on him," said his best friend Steven.

"That's a great idea," Jason replied.

Just after midnight, Marvin drifted off to sleep. Steven and Jason looked at each other and nodded. Steven slipped out of his sleeping bag and hid in Marvin's closet. Jason lay still next to his friend and pretended to be asleep. After a moment Steven began to tap gently on the closet door. Marvin stirred gently. Then Steven continued and tapped even harder from behind the door. Marvin sprang from his sleep and sat upright. As the noise continued, he struggled to understand where it was coming from.

"Jason," he whispered. "Do you hear that sound?"

Jason pretended to wake from a deep sleep.

"What's wrong Marvin?" he asked.

"Do you hear that noise?" Marvin asked again.

Jason struggled to keep a smile off his face.

"Yes," Jason replied nervously. "I think it's coming from behind the closet door."

Marvin gulped as fear gripped his body. He climbed from his bed and stepped towards the closet. He began to freeze up as he got closer to the door. His trembling hand reached out towards the door. Just as he was about to push the door open, Steven leapt out from behind the door and shouted loudly. Marvin shrieked, jumped backwards, and fell onto the sleeping bags.

"Do you believe in ghosts now?" Jason asked with a giggle.

Marvin shook his head. He tried to look annoyed, but he couldn't help smiling. Steven was laughing out loud as he sat on a nearby chair. Marvin started to laugh as well.

"Of course he does," Steven said. "But I bet he didn't expect his own house to be haunted!"

"Fine, you got me," Marvin admitted. "For just a minute, I was scared. Nice one guys. Now let's get some sleep. And no more tricking."

Steven and Jason both promised they were done with tricking. But Marvin decided to leave the lamp on just in case.

52 In the sentence below, the word <u>pale</u> shows that the light was –

> **They would gather in his bedroom and sit in pale lamplight talking about ghosts and goblins.**

Ⓐ   bright

Ⓑ   clear

Ⓒ   dim

Ⓓ   warm

53 What does the photograph of Marvin at the start of the passage mainly suggest about him?

Ⓐ   He is not afraid of anything.

Ⓑ   He is known for playing jokes.

Ⓒ   He is more scared than he admits.

Ⓓ   He is about to have a prank played on him.

54 Place the events from the passage in order by writing the numbers 1, 2, 3, and 4 in front of each sentence.

_____   Steven hides in the closet.

_____   Marvin falls asleep.

_____   Steven suggests playing a trick.

_____   Jason asks Marvin if he believes in ghosts.

55 Read this sentence from the passage.

Just after midnight, Marvin drifted off to sleep.

What mood does the phrase "drifted off" create?

Ⓐ   Curious

Ⓑ   Calm

Ⓒ   Playful

Ⓓ   Hopeful

56 Circle **three** words the author uses in paragraph 12 to emphasize how scared Marvin felt.

gulped   gripped   climbed   stepped

closet   trembling   reached   leapt

57 Describe the role that Steven and Jason play during the trick.

Steven:

_____

_____

Jason:

_____

_____

58 Why does Marvin jump backwards and fall onto the sleeping bags?

    Ⓐ   Steven pushes him.

    Ⓑ   Steven scares him.

    Ⓒ   He is angry with Steven.

    Ⓓ   He wants to go back to sleep.

59 Why does the author most likely use the word <u>sprang</u> instead of <u>woke</u> in the sentence below?

Marvin sprang from his sleep and sat upright.

    Ⓐ   To show that Marvin knows about the trick

    Ⓑ   To show that Marvin feels sleepy

    Ⓒ   To show that Marvin had a bad dream

    Ⓓ   To show that Marvin woke suddenly

60 After Marvin hears a noise, the author says that Jason "struggled to keep a smile off his face." Explain why Jason has to stop himself from smiling.

_____

_____

_____

_____

_____

61 Choose **two** sentences from the paragraph below that create suspense. Circle the **two** sentences below. Then explain why you chose those sentences.

Marvin gulped as fear gripped his body. He climbed from his bed and stepped towards the closet. He began to freeze up as he got closer to the door. His trembling hand reached out towards the door. Just as he was about to push the door open, Steven leapt out from behind the door and shouted loudly. Marvin shrieked, jumped backwards, and fell onto the sleeping bags.

_____

_____

_____

_____

_____

_____

62   Do you think the trick that Steven and Jason played was mean or funny? Use details from the passage to support your opinion.

_____

_____

_____

_____

_____

63   Think about how Marvin seems to feel about the trick. Circle the sentence that describes how you think he feels about the trick.

It was mean.   It was funny.

Give **two** details that help show whether he thinks the trick was mean or funny.

1: _____

_____

2: _____

_____

The passage below contains errors. The words or phrases that are incorrect are underlined. For each word or phrase underlined, answer the question below.

Beach Day

I love going to the beach! There aren't many things better to take your mind off the world than just <u>lieing</u> around and doing not much of anything at all. You <u>will</u> wander along the edge of the ocean and enjoy the feel of your feet sinking into the cool sand. I sometimes stop to watch the rhythm of the waves as <u>it</u> roll in.

Whenever I'm relaxing at the beach, I lay <u>their</u> for hours and let my mind wander. All I need is a big old shady palm tree, a beach towel, a sandy beach, and some peace and quiet. It doesn't get <u>more</u> better than that! In fact, there is not a single place in the <u>hole</u> world that I would rather be!

64 Which of these should replace <u>lieing</u>?

   Ⓐ   liing

   Ⓑ   lying

   Ⓒ   lyeing

   Ⓓ   liying

65 Which of these should replace <u>will</u>?

   Ⓐ   must

   Ⓑ   can

   Ⓒ   do

   Ⓓ   are

66   Which of these should replace <u>it</u>?

    Ⓐ   that

    Ⓑ   them

    Ⓒ   they

    Ⓓ   this

67   As it is used in the sentence, what is the correct spelling of <u>their</u>? Write your answer below.

_____

68   Which of these should replace <u>more</u>?

    Ⓐ   most

    Ⓑ   very

    Ⓒ   much

    Ⓓ   either

69   As it is used in the sentence, what is the correct spelling of <u>hole</u>? Write your answer below.

_____

The questions below are answered after listening to a passage. Ask someone to read you the passage "A Fresh Coat of Paint" from the back of this book. Then answer the questions below.

Questions for "A Fresh Coat of Paint"

70   What is the main problem in the passage?

Ⓐ   They do not mix the paint properly.

Ⓑ   They do not know how to paint a bedroom.

Ⓒ   They cannot decide what color to paint the bedroom.

Ⓓ   They cannot find enough yellow or blue paint.

71   What color does the bedroom get painted?

Ⓐ   Yellow

Ⓑ   Blue

Ⓒ   Green

Ⓓ   Red

72   How does the narrator feel about her painted bedroom?

Ⓐ   Pleased

Ⓑ   Annoyed

Ⓒ   Confused

Ⓓ   Worried

The questions below are answered after listening to a passage. Ask someone to read you the passage "A Helping Hand" from the back of this book. Then answer the questions below.

Questions for "A Helping Hand"

73   The speaker's main purpose in the passage was probably to –

     Ⓐ   encourage people to become doctors

     Ⓑ   describe the life of Dr. Price

     Ⓒ   inspire people to try to make a difference

     Ⓓ   explain to readers why Dr. Price is often away

74   What does the speaker most admire about Dr. Price?

     Ⓐ   How he is a successful doctor

     Ⓑ   How he travels the world

     Ⓒ   How he helps others

     Ⓓ   How he is wealthy

75   What does the title of the passage most likely refer to?

     Ⓐ   How doctors use their hands to heal

     Ⓑ   How Dr. Price wants to help people

     Ⓒ   How not all people have access to healthcare

     Ⓓ   How many people are needed when disasters occur

END OF SESSION 2

Florida Standards Assessment

English Language Arts

Practice Test 2

Session 1

Instructions

Read each passage and answer the questions that follow it.

For each multiple-choice question, fill in the circle for the correct answer. For other types of questions, follow the instructions given. Some of the questions require a written answer. Write your answer on the lines provided.

The Taming of the Lion

The lion had a fearful roar
that scared all who dared to follow.
It made his victims run and hide,
and pray for their tomorrow.

His mane was as glorious as sunshine,
and framed his handsome face.
His lair was known to all around
as a truly frightening place.

Until he met a maiden,
and fell hopelessly in love.
His roar became a whisper,
a soft sound to birds above.

His lair was soon a palace,
a kindly home of gentle calm,
where he would hold his loved ones,
and make sure they met no harm.

The lion never harmed another,
or chased his worried prey.
Instead they lived in harmony
and shared each summer's day.

He had been tamed within an instant
by the gentle hand of love,
that would keep him calm forever
beneath the flight of gentle doves.

1 Read this line from the poem.

The lion had a fearful roar

What does the word <u>fearful</u> mean?

Ⓐ   Without fear

Ⓑ   Having fear

Ⓒ   More fear

Ⓓ   Less fear

2 According to the poem, why does the lion become tamer?

Ⓐ   He gets older.

Ⓑ   He falls in love.

Ⓒ   He has children.

Ⓓ   He starts feeling lonely.

3 What is the rhyme pattern of each stanza of the poem?

Ⓐ   The second and fourth lines rhyme.

Ⓑ   There are two pairs of rhyming lines.

Ⓒ   The first and last lines rhyme.

Ⓓ   None of the lines rhyme.

4   Select the line from the poem that contains a simile.

☐   *The lion had a fearful roar*

☐   *that scared all who dared to follow.*

☐   *It made his victims run and hide,*

☐   *and pray for their tomorrow.*

☐   *His mane was as glorious as sunshine,*

☐   *and framed his handsome face.*

☐   *His lair was known to all around*

☐   *as a truly frightening place.*

5   Describe the meaning of the simile identified in Question 4. In your answer, explain what the simile helps you imagine.

_____

_____

_____

_____

_____

_____

6   Which word best describes the tone of the poem?

    Ⓐ   Funny

    Ⓑ   Serious

    Ⓒ   Sweet

    Ⓓ   Tense

7   Read this line from the poem.

    a soft sound to birds above

The alliteration in this line mainly creates a feeling of –

    Ⓐ   uneasiness

    Ⓑ   surprise

    Ⓒ   calm

    Ⓓ   fear

8   The poem states that the lion had been tamed "within an instant." What does the phrase "within an instant" mean?

    Ⓐ   Very well

    Ⓑ   Unusually

    Ⓒ   Suddenly

    Ⓓ   Over a long time

9 Read this line from the poem.

His roar became a whisper,

What does this change show about the lion?

Ⓐ   He has become shy.

Ⓑ   He is no longer scary.

Ⓒ   He feels afraid.

Ⓓ   He listens to others.

10 What does the imagery in the lines below help the reader understand?

**It made his victims run and hide,
and pray for their tomorrow.**

Ⓐ   Where the lion lives

Ⓑ   How feared the lion is

Ⓒ   Why the lion dislikes people

Ⓓ   How strong and fast the lion is

11 How many stanzas does the poem have? Circle the correct answer.

2   3   4   6   8   12   20   24

12 Which pair of lines from the poem explain what causes the lion to change?

   Ⓐ   *His mane was as glorious as sunshine,*

        and framed his handsome face.

   Ⓑ   *Until he met a maiden,*

        and fell hopelessly in love.

   Ⓒ   *His lair was soon a palace,*

        a kindly home of gentle calm,

   Ⓓ   *The lion never harmed another,*

        or chased his worried prey.

13 Compare the language used to describe the lion at the start of the poem with the language used at the end of the poem. Complete the table below by listing **three** more examples of words or phrases the poet uses to show what the lion is like before and after he changes.

Words to Show the Lion is Feared	Words to Show the Lion is Harmless
dared to follow	palace
victims	gentle calm

One Game for Two

Thomas could be quite mean at times. He had a younger brother called Simon and he rarely shared his toys with him.

"You must share Thomas," urged his mother. "One day you will want somebody to share something with you and they won't. Then you will be very upset."

Thomas just laughed his mother's advice off.

"I'll be fine, Mom," he replied. "As long as I have my own toys, I will always be fine."

His mother just shrugged her shoulders.

"Very well," she said. "It seems that you know best."

One day she decided to teach him a lesson. Both boys had been begging for a video game system for over a year. She decided that it was finally time to buy the boys the video game system and a few games.

When Christmas day arrived, both boys were patiently waiting for their presents in front of the fireplace. As Thomas tore into the video game package, his eyes lit up. It was the exact video game system he had wanted for so long.

Simon took longer than Thomas to carefully unwrap his own present. When he did, he was delighted to see three video games. He thanked his mother for not just getting him one great game, but getting him three.

Thomas raced over to check out the games. He saw they were the games he wanted as well and grinned.

"There is just one thing, Simon," Simon's mother said. "You don't have a system to play them on, so you're going to have to ask if you can use your brother's." Thomas's smile turned quickly into a frown.

"But it's my present," Thomas said gruffly. "I don't want him to use it."

"I think you should be kinder and let your brother use it," his mother suggested.

"Do I have to?" Thomas whined.

"You don't have to," his mother said. "But it would be the right thing to do."

Thomas just shrugged. Then he shook his head.

"No," he said firmly. "I've wanted it for ages and I don't want him to break it."

Simon looked at his brother sadly. He wasn't surprised by his decision, but he was still upset by it.

"Very well," the mother said. "But I hope you realize you won't have much fun with your video game system without any games to play."

Thomas suddenly realized that Simon had games, but he didn't. Simon started to say that Thomas could play his games, but his mother stopped him.

"Since you don't want to share your system with Simon, it wouldn't be fair for you to play his games," the mother continued.

Now Thomas realized that he had a problem. He had the system, Simon had the games, and they needed both to be able to play.

Thomas paused and thought for a moment.

"Okay, I suppose I could share my video game system," he whispered quietly. "That does seem fair."

Simon quickly agreed to share his games and they spent the rest of the day playing a racing game together.

14 Read this sentence from the passage.

> **He had a younger brother called Simon and he rarely shared his toys with him.**

Which word means the opposite of <u>rarely</u>?

  Ⓐ   Sometimes

  Ⓑ   Never

  Ⓒ   Often

  Ⓓ   Once

15 Read this sentence from the passage.

> **As Thomas tore into the video game package, his eyes lit up.**

The word <u>tore</u> suggests that Simon opened the package –

  Ⓐ   slowly

  Ⓑ   roughly

  Ⓒ   carefully

  Ⓓ   calmly

16   According to the passage, how is Simon different from Thomas?

    Ⓐ   He is selfish.

    Ⓑ   He is older.

    Ⓒ   He is kinder.

    Ⓓ   He is wiser.

17   Based on your answer to Question 16, describe **two** details that show what Simon is like.

    1: _____

    _____

    2: _____

    _____

18   Why does Thomas most likely grin when he sees the video games?

    Ⓐ   He knows that Simon wanted them.

    Ⓑ   He doesn't want to show that he is upset.

    Ⓒ   He thinks that he will be able to play them.

    Ⓓ   He expects his present to be the same.

19   The main theme of the passage is about –

Ⓐ   getting along with your siblings

Ⓑ   sharing your things with others

Ⓒ   buying good presents

Ⓓ   thinking of clever plans

20   Which sentence best supports your answer to Question 19?

Ⓐ   *One day you will want somebody to share something with you and they won't.*

Ⓑ   *One day she decided to teach him a lesson.*

Ⓒ   *Both boys had been begging for a video game system for over a year.*

Ⓓ   *I've wanted it for ages and I don't want him to break it.*

21   Circle the word below that best describes Thomas's mother. Explain why you made that choice.

mean   clever

_____

_____

_____

_____

_____

22   Why does Thomas finally decide to share his present with Simon? In what way is his decision still selfish? Use details from the passage to explain your answer.

_____

_____

_____

_____

_____

23   Read this sentence from the passage.

As Thomas tore into the video game package, his eyes lit up.

Explain what the phrase "his eyes lit up" shows about Thomas.

_____

_____

_____

_____

24 Read this section of the passage.

> Thomas's smile turned quickly into a frown.
>
> "But it's my present," Thomas said gruffly. "I don't want him to use it."
>
> "I think you should be kinder and let your brother use it," his mother suggested.
>
> "Do I have to?" Thomas whined.
>
> "You don't have to," his mother said. "But it would be the right thing to do."
>
> Thomas just shrugged. Then he shook his head.
>
> "No," he said firmly. "I've wanted it for ages and I don't want him to break it."

Circle **three** words that show that Thomas is grumpy. On the lines below, explain why you chose those words.

_____

_____

_____

_____

_____

_____

The West Moor Sports Camp

The health of our children is important. Good health means eating well and being active. Children should take part in sports or other activities often. This isn't always easy. In cities, it can be hard to find activities to do. Don't be alarmed, though. The West Moor Sports Camp can help!

The West Moor Sports Camp is an outdoor camp for people of all ages. Children can enjoy outdoor activities. They can also make new friends. All while the parents relax, knowing that their children are safe.

The West Moor Sports Camp is located among lush fields. There is a lot of open space for youngsters to run around and enjoy themselves. There are many games and sports that they can take part in. These include football, soccer, baseball, basketball, athletics, and tennis. They can also take part in activities on the lake like rowing and sailing. There are also fitness classes that children can take part in.

There are many benefits to the camp. The first is that children will take part in a fitness program that they will enjoy! They will become fitter while having fun! The second is that children will make new friends. They will learn how to work with other children. It may also help children develop good fitness habits. Finally, children will have the chance to try activities they might never have been able to do before. Children can have a go at everything. With so many to choose from, they might find the sport or hobby that is just right for them.

Many children find that they enjoy playing sports. They leave our camp with a new appreciation for being outdoors and being active. It becomes a new interest. In the age of computer games, this is a great thing!

So visit our website today to find out more. Give your children a better future!

25   Read this sentence from the passage.

In cities, it can be hard to find activities to do.

Which word means the opposite of <u>hard</u>?

Ⓐ   Cheap

Ⓑ   Difficult

Ⓒ   Easy

Ⓓ   Costly

26   In the first paragraph, what does the word <u>alarmed</u> mean?

Ⓐ   Worried

Ⓑ   Lazy

Ⓒ   Confused

Ⓓ   Silly

27   How is the first paragraph mainly organized?

Ⓐ   A problem is described and then a solution is given.

Ⓑ   Events are described in the order they occur.

Ⓒ   Facts are given to support an argument.

Ⓓ   A question is asked and then answered.

28 The first paragraph states that children "should take part in sports or other activities often." How does the camp encourage children to do this? Use at least **two** details from the passage in your answer.

_____

_____

_____

_____

_____

29 Use details from the passage to complete the web below.

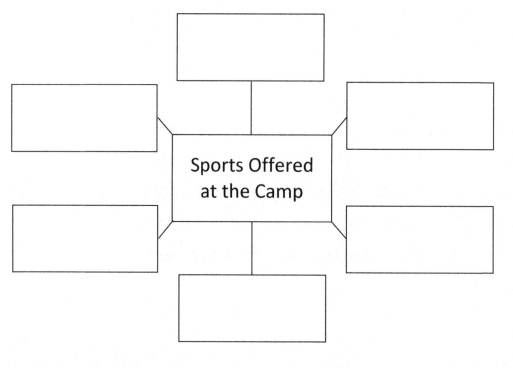

30 The photograph is probably included mainly as an example of children –

Ⓐ   being looked after

Ⓑ   making new friends

Ⓒ   solving problems

Ⓓ   working together

31 Which question is the passage mainly intended to answer?

Ⓐ   When was the West Moor Sports Camp started?

Ⓑ   What skills do young people need to develop?

Ⓒ   Why should children attend the West Moor Sports Camp?

Ⓓ   Will the West Moor Sports Camp be safe for kids?

32 According to the passage, what should you do to find out more about the camp?

Ⓐ   Request a brochure

Ⓑ   Telephone the camp

Ⓒ   Attend an open day

Ⓓ   Visit the camp's website

33 Look at the diagram below. Complete the diagram by listing **two** more benefits of the camp.

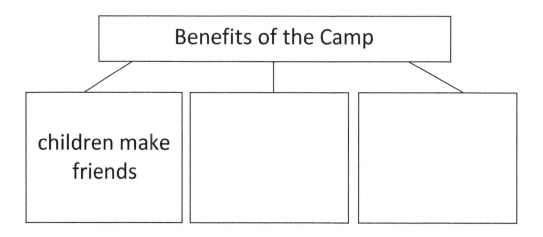

34 Is the information given about the camp biased toward making the camp sound good? Explain your answer.

_____

_____

_____

_____

_____

_____

The passage below contains errors. The words or phrases that are incorrect are underlined. For each word or phrase underlined, answer the question below.

Letter to the Editor

Dear Editor,

I am worried that our town park does not look as nice as it once did. It is not as well-cared for and is not cleaned as often. There <u>is</u> food wrappers, cans, and even <u>breaked</u> glass lying around. I've noticed that there is a lot of graffiti <u>appeering</u> too.

I think that something <u>may</u> be done about this right away! It is no longer a lovely place to spend the afternoon. It is not even a safe place <u>to played</u> with all the trash lying around. <u>The park is rarely used now but that could all change.</u> We just need some action taken to fix the problems.

Yours with hope,

Evan

35 Which of these should replace <u>is</u>?

    Ⓐ   are

    Ⓑ   be

    Ⓒ   been

    Ⓓ   was

36 Write the correct past tense of <u>break</u> that should replace the word <u>breaked</u>. Write your answer below.

_____

37 Which of these should replace <u>appeering</u>?

   Ⓐ   apeering

   Ⓑ   apearing

   Ⓒ   appearing

   Ⓓ   appering

38 Which of these should replace <u>may</u>?

   Ⓐ   can

   Ⓑ   would

   Ⓒ   must

   Ⓓ   shall

39 Which of these should replace <u>to played</u>?

   Ⓐ   to play

   Ⓑ   to playing

   Ⓒ   to had played

   Ⓓ   to will have played

40 Which of these places the comma in the correct place?

   Ⓐ   The park is rarely used, now but that could all change.

   Ⓑ   The park is rarely used now, but that could all change.

   Ⓒ   The park is rarely used now but, that could all change.

   Ⓓ   The park is rarely used now but that could, all change.

END OF SESSION 1

Florida Standards Assessment

English Language Arts

Practice Test 2

Session 2

Instructions

Read each passage and answer the questions that follow it.

For each multiple-choice question, fill in the circle for the correct answer. For other types of questions, follow the instructions given. Some of the questions require a written answer. Write your answer on the lines provided.

Abraham Lincoln

Abraham Lincoln was the 16th President of the United States. He was born in 1809. He died on April 15, 1865. Lincoln served the United States as President for just short of five years. He is remembered for his strong leadership skills. He led the nation through several conflicts, including the American Civil War.

Abraham Lincoln was born into a poor family. He was mostly self-educated. He worked as a country lawyer. During this period of his life, he also started a family. He raised four children.

His career in politics began at the state level. He was fiercely against slavery. He fought it through national debates. He gave public speeches about the issue. He wrote letters to persuade others to agree with him. His strong opinion won him the support of many. He was then elected president in 1860.

In April 1861, the American Civil War began. Lincoln planned to defeat the South. He wanted to reunify the nation. He oversaw the war effort very closely. He skillfully prevented British support for the South in late 1861. He took control of the civil conflict during the next two years. In 1863, he issued an order that ended slavery. Over 3 million slaves were freed. The war came to an end in 1865. Lincoln achieved his goal of uniting the nation.

Abraham Lincoln was shot and killed just six days after the end of the war. It was a sad end for a man who achieved so much. Abraham Lincoln is thought of by many as the greatest president of all time.

41   Read this sentence from the passage.

He was fiercely against slavery.

As it is used in the sentence, what does the word <u>fiercely</u> mean?

Ⓐ   Usually

Ⓑ   Quickly

Ⓒ   Strongly

Ⓓ   Strangely

42   Read this sentence from the passage.

He wanted to reunify the nation.

If the word <u>unify</u> means "to bring together," what does the word <u>reunify</u> mean?

Ⓐ   To bring together more

Ⓑ   To bring back together

Ⓒ   To stop bringing together

Ⓓ   To bring together before

43 In which year did Abraham Lincoln become president? Circle the correct answer.

1860   1861   1862   1863   1864   1865

44 Which paragraph has the main purpose of describing Abraham Lincoln's achievements during the war?

    Ⓐ   Paragraph 1

    Ⓑ   Paragraph 2

    Ⓒ   Paragraph 4

    Ⓓ   Paragraph 5

45 In which sentence from the passage does the author give a personal opinion about Lincoln?

    Ⓐ   *Abraham Lincoln was the 16th President of the United States.*

    Ⓑ   *In 1863, he issued an order that ended slavery.*

    Ⓒ   *Abraham Lincoln was shot and killed just six days after the end of the war.*

    Ⓓ   *It was a sad end for a man who achieved so much.*

46   Which detail about Abraham Lincoln is least important to understanding why he is considered by some as the greatest president of all time?

   Ⓐ   He achieved his goal of unifying the nation.

   Ⓑ   He fought to end slavery.

   Ⓒ   He was born into a poor family.

   Ⓓ   He led America through the Civil War.

47   Complete the web below using information from the passage.

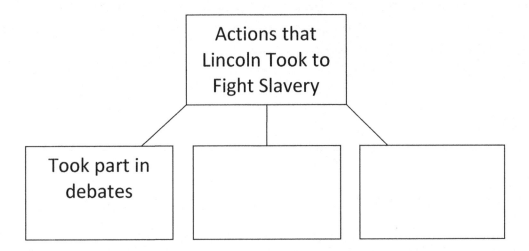

48 The passage describes Abraham Lincoln's achievements. Describe **two** of Lincoln's achievements.

1: _____

_____

2: _____

_____

49 The passage describes how Lincoln was born into a poor family and was mostly self-educated. Describe how these details affect how you feel about his achievements.

_____

_____

_____

_____

_____

_____

_____

_____

The Girlfriend and the Mother

Prince Arnold had a very close bond with his mother. They shared everything with each other. They had remained close since he had been a child. One day, he met a girl named Chloe and she became his girlfriend. Gradually, Arnold began to spend more time with his girlfriend than with his mother.

Although he still enjoyed long conversations with his mother, she began to feel left out. She felt that the only time she would get to spend with him was in the evenings. This was when he would fall asleep on the couch and she would sit beside him and stroke his hair.

His mother really liked the gray strands that grew in his hair. She felt they made him look wise. So as she stroked his head she would remove some of the darker hairs from his scalp. She did this over many nights for an entire year.

Arnold's girlfriend had a similar habit. She thought that his gray hairs made him look old. So she would pluck as many gray hairs from his head as she possibly could. She too did this for many nights over the year.

After a year had gone by, Arnold found that he was almost completely bald. His mother and girlfriend had removed so much of his hair that he was left only with short little tufts. Both women and Arnold were unhappy with his new look. The ladies felt that their battle for his time had led to the problem.

"We're so sorry," they said. "What we have done is unfair."

They realized that they must all get along and spend time together if they were to remain happy. The mother and the girlfriend made a promise to be happy sharing Prince Arnold's time.

50   Read this sentence from the passage.

His mother and girlfriend had removed so much of his hair that he was left only with short little tufts.

What does the word <u>removed</u> mean?

Ⓐ   Scared off

Ⓑ   Fought over

Ⓒ   Taken away

Ⓓ   Changed places

51   Read this sentence from the passage.

Prince Arnold had a very close bond with his mother.

Which meaning of the word <u>bond</u> is used in the sentence?

Ⓐ   To connect two or more items

Ⓑ   A relationship or link between people

Ⓒ   An agreement or promise

Ⓓ   A type of glue

52   What is the mother's main problem in the passage?

    Ⓐ   She dislikes her son's hair.

    Ⓑ   She does not want to share her son.

    Ⓒ   She argues with her son.

    Ⓓ   She wants her son to get married.

53   "The Girlfriend and the Mother" is most like a –

    Ⓐ   true story

    Ⓑ   science fiction story

    Ⓒ   biography

    Ⓓ   fable

54   How are the girlfriend and the mother alike?

    Ⓐ   They are both pleased when Arnold is bald.

    Ⓑ   They both pluck out Arnold's hair.

    Ⓒ   They both dislike Arnold's gray hair.

    Ⓓ   They have both known Arnold since he was young.

55   How does the mother change in the passage?

    Ⓐ   She realizes that her son is a grown man.

    Ⓑ   She accepts her son's relationship with Chloe.

    Ⓒ   She loses interest in her son.

    Ⓓ   She learns that Chloe is a nice person.

56   Complete these sentences. Write **one** of the words below on each line.

royal   kind   old   unusual

wise   silly   young   special

Chloe thinks that Arnold's gray hair makes him look _____.

Arnold's mother thinks that his gray hair makes him look _____.

57   Based on your answer to Question 56, describe how their different feelings affect their actions.

_____

_____

_____

_____

_____

_____

58   What will the mother most likely do next?

    Ⓐ   Come up with a plan to break up her son and Chloe

    Ⓑ   Start making an effort to spend time with her son and Chloe

    Ⓒ   Make her son think that his baldness is Chloe's fault

    Ⓓ   Start spending time with her husband instead of her son

59   How do you think Arnold feels at the end of the passage? Use details from the passage to explain why you think Arnold feels that way.

    _____

    _____

    _____

    _____

    _____

    _____

60 Use details from the passage to complete the cause and effect diagram below.

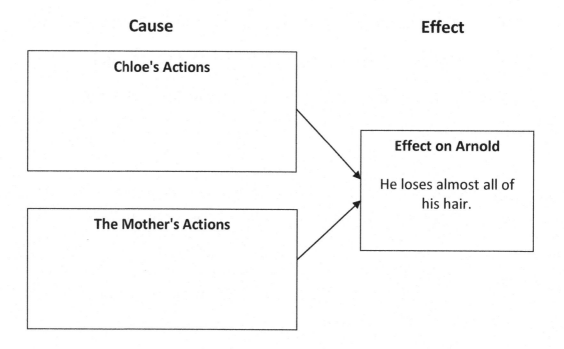

Cause

Effect

Chloe's Actions

The Mother's Actions

Effect on Arnold

He loses almost all of his hair.

61 Describe what the art in the passage represents. Use details from the passage to support your answer.

_____

_____

_____

_____

_____

_____

The passage below contains errors. The words or phrases that are incorrect are underlined. For each word or phrase underlined, answer the question below.

Camels

Camels can survive for long periods of time without drinking water. The camel's hump plays a big <u>roll</u>. However, it does not store water like many people think. It <u>actuelly</u> stores fat. The fat is used as a source of energy. Camels do store water. <u>They store it in their bodies. In their blood too.</u>

Camels can go longer than 7 days without drinking. When they do find water, they <u>will taking</u> a lot in. They are able to consume over 50 gallons of water at a time! These features allow them to survive in the desert. Camels <u>was</u> once found in <u>north america</u>. They are now mainly found in the deserts of the African and Arabian regions.

62   As it is used in the sentence, what is the correct spelling of <u>roll</u>? Write your answer below.

_____

63   Which of these should replace <u>actuelly</u>?

    Ⓐ   actualy

    Ⓑ   actuely

    Ⓒ   actually

    Ⓓ   actully

64 What is the best way to combine the sentences?

Ⓐ They store it in their bodies, in their blood too.

Ⓑ They store it in their bodies, in blood too.

Ⓒ They store it in their bodies and in their blood.

Ⓓ They store it in their bodies their blood.

65 Which of these should replace <u>will taking</u>?

Ⓐ will take

Ⓑ have taken

Ⓒ would have taken

Ⓓ will took

66 What is the correct way to capitalize <u>north america</u>? Write your answer below.

_____

67 Which of these should replace <u>was</u>?

Ⓐ is

Ⓑ are

Ⓒ were

Ⓓ which

The questions below are answered after listening to a passage. Ask someone to read you the passage "The Little Things" from the back of this book. Then answer the questions below.

Questions for "The Little Things"

68   Which phrase from the passage creates a mood of calm?

Ⓐ   *throw up his arms*

Ⓑ   *always bellow loudly*

Ⓒ   *dressed in his overalls*

Ⓓ   *strolled out to his garden*

69   Patrick would most likely describe his life as –

Ⓐ   difficult and exhausting

Ⓑ   exciting and carefree

Ⓒ   dull and disappointing

Ⓓ   simple but rewarding

70   What is the main theme of the passage about?

Ⓐ   Enjoying what you have

Ⓑ   Growing your own food

Ⓒ   Having a daily routine

Ⓓ   Forgetting your troubles

The questions below are answered after listening to a passage. Ask someone to read you the passage "Recycling" from the back of this book. Then answer the questions below.

Questions for "Recycling"

71 Complete the web below using information from the passage.

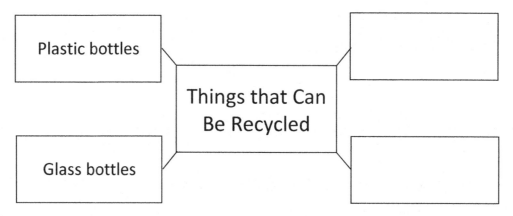

72 What is the main purpose of the passage?

   Ⓐ   To tell a story about recycling

   Ⓑ   To explain how items are recycled

   Ⓒ   To teach people how to recycle paper

   Ⓓ   To persuade people to recycle

73 Which sentence from the passage best summarizes the main message?

   Ⓐ   *Recycling helps keep our planet healthy.*

   Ⓑ   *They are broken down and then used to make new things.*

   Ⓒ   *This is good because the new things take much less energy to make.*

   Ⓓ   *It also decreases the amount of waste.*

END OF SESSION 2

Florida Standards Assessment

English Language Arts

Practice Test 3

Session 1

Instructions

Read each passage and answer the questions that follow it.

For each multiple-choice question, fill in the circle for the correct answer. For other types of questions, follow the instructions given. Some of the questions require a written answer. Write your answer on the lines provided.

Robert De Niro

Robert De Niro is an American actor. He is known as one of the finest actors of his time. He has starred in a number of blockbuster films. He has also won many awards.

He was born in 1943 in New York City. De Niro left high school at the age of sixteen. He wanted to have a career in acting. He dreamed of appearing in Hollywood films. He studied acting between 1959 and 1963. He then took part in several small films.

His first major film role arrived in 1973. It was in the film *Bang the Drum Slowly*. After this, he won a role in the film *The Godfather Part II*. The film is one of the greatest films in history. He won the Academy Award for Best Supporting Actor for this role. It was the start of a great career. He was then given the lead role in many films.

During this time, he became good friends with Martin Scorsese. Scorsese was a successful director. They began to work together often. Their first film together was *Mean Streets* in 1973. De Niro won the Academy Award for Best Actor for this role. In 1980, he starred in the film *Raging Bull*. Scorsese was the director again. And again, De Niro won an Academy Award. They have worked on a number of box office hits over the years including *Casino*, *Cape Fear*, and *The Departed*.

His career continued. Over three decades, he has starred in many films. These have even included comedies like *Meet the Parents* and *Analyze This*.

In 2011, he was awarded a Golden Globe called the Cecil B. DeMille Award. This award is given for "outstanding contributions to the world of entertainment." Winners of the award in other years have included some great actors and directors including Steven Spielberg, Harrison Ford, Morgan Freeman, and Jodie Foster. It is also another achievement he shared with Martin Scorsese. Scorsese received the award in 2010.

Robert De Niro Films

Year	Title
1973	Bang the Drum Slowly
1974	The Godfather Part II
1976	Taxi Driver
1977	New York, New York
1980	Raging Bull
1986	The Mission
1987	The Untouchables
1988	Midnight Run
1990	Goodfellas
1991	Backdraft
1991	Cape Fear
1993	A Bronx Tale
1995	Casino
1995	Heat
1998	Ronin
1999	Analyze This
2000	Meet the Parents
2002	Showtime
2006	The Good Shepherd
2006	The Departed
2009	Everybody's Fine
2011	Limitless
2012	Silver Linings Playbook
2013	Last Vegas

Fun Fact

There is one other surprising link between De Niro and Scorsese. They were both the voices of characters in the 2004 animated comedy film *Shark Tale*. De Niro is the voice of a shark and Scorsese is the voice of a pufferfish!

1   As it is used in paragraph 1, what does <u>finest</u> mean?

   Ⓐ   Best

   Ⓑ   Smallest

   Ⓒ   Rarest

   Ⓓ   Nicest

2   Which of these does the table best show?

   Ⓐ   How many awards De Niro has won

   Ⓑ   How many times De Niro worked with Scorsese

   Ⓒ   How long De Niro has been acting for

   Ⓓ   How De Niro chooses his roles

3   Describe **two** more things the table shows about De Niro and his career.

   1: _____

   _____

   2: _____

   _____

4 Determine whether each sentence in paragraph 3 is a fact or an opinion. Write F or O on each line to show your choice.

_____ His first major film role arrived in 1973.

_____ It was in the film *Bang the Drum Slowly*.

_____ After this, he won a role in the film *The Godfather Part II*.

_____ The film is one of the greatest films in history.

_____ He won the Academy Award for Best Supporting Actor for this role.

_____ It was the start of a great career.

_____ He was then given the lead role in many films.

5 How is the passage mainly organized?

Ⓐ A solution to a problem is described.

Ⓑ A question is asked and then answered.

Ⓒ A series of events are described in order.

Ⓓ Two different actors are compared.

6 The passage was probably written mainly to –

Ⓐ encourage people to become actors

Ⓑ describe the life of Robert De Niro

Ⓒ tell a funny story about a movie star

Ⓓ teach readers how to break into films

7   According to the passage, how are Robert De Niro and Martin Scorsese similar?

   Ⓐ   They were both born in New York.

   Ⓑ   They are both good actors.

   Ⓒ   They both direct movies.

   Ⓓ   They are both successful.

8   Based on your answer to Question 7, describe **two** details given in the passage that support your answer.

   1: _____

   _____

   2: _____

   _____

9   How would this passage be different if it were an autobiography?

   Ⓐ   It would be a more factual summary of De Niro's life.

   Ⓑ   It would include references to prove the statements made.

   Ⓒ   It would include quotes from other sources.

   Ⓓ   It would be De Niro's account of his own life.

10 Give **two** details the author includes to support the idea that De Niro and Scorsese are a good team.

Supporting Detail 1:

_____

_____

Supporting Detail 2:

_____

_____

11 Read this sentence about winners of the Cecil B. DeMille Award.

> **Winners of the award in other years have included some great actors and directors including Steven Spielberg, Harrison Ford, Morgan Freeman, and Jodie Foster.**

What does this sentence help you understand about the significance of De Niro receiving the award?

_____

_____

_____

_____

_____

12 How does the author show that Robert De Niro is a successful actor? Use at least **three** details from the passage to support your answer.

_____

_____

_____

_____

_____

_____

_____

_____

_____

_____

_____

_____

_____

_____

Catching Up

June 15, 2013

Dear Sally,

I am writing to see how you are doing at college. Are you settling in well? I remember how upset you got when we dropped you off. I hate to think of you as being unhappy. I know what a bright and cheerful girl you are. It is hard to imagine you any other way! I am sure that you have already made a lot of new friends. How are your courses going? Are you enjoying the work and learning a lot? I bet you are finding it very interesting. I am so proud of you for studying and working your way toward your goals. It is motivating me in my own studies.

Everything is fine at home. I am halfway through my exams and have been enjoying them so far. I am prepared and relaxed when I attend each one. So far, they have all been a piece of cake. If all goes well, I may even be following in your footsteps in a few years time. We could even find ourselves at the same college. Having said that, I am not sure how much work we would actually get done! Knowing us we would either be having too much fun or wasting time with silly arguments. Seriously though, I really miss our chats.

Dad and Mom are great as always. Dad is working hard at his new job. It is going very well, and he may even have to travel to London soon. Mom is trying to get fit for our summer vacation. I know you can't make it, but you will be sorely missed. I am hoping that you will be able to make it back next year to travel with us. Any trip abroad is just not the same without you! I do understand, though. I know you are working hard and that it is all for your future.

Please write back to me when you get the chance. Until then, you will remain in my thoughts.

Lots of love,

Rory

13 Read this sentence from the passage.

I am prepared and relaxed when I attend each one.

Which word could best be used in place of <u>prepared</u>?

Ⓐ   Calm

Ⓑ   Ready

Ⓒ   Studied

Ⓓ   Patient

14 As it is used in the sentence below, what does <u>sorely</u> mean?

I know you can't make it, but you will be sorely missed.

Ⓐ   Certainly

Ⓑ   Suddenly

Ⓒ   Sadly

Ⓓ   Greatly

15 What is the second paragraph mostly about?

Ⓐ   What Rory has been doing at home

Ⓑ   What Rory imagines his sister is doing

Ⓒ   Why Rory misses his sister

Ⓓ   What Rory plans to do after school

16   Read this sentence from the passage.

So far, they have all been a piece of cake.

The phrase "a piece of cake" means that something is —

Ⓐ   easy

Ⓑ   tasty

Ⓒ   quick

Ⓓ   funny

17   The reader can conclude that Sally is Rory's —

Ⓐ   older sister

Ⓑ   younger sister

Ⓒ   twin sister

Ⓓ   mother

18   Think about how Rory feels about his sister not being able to go on the family vacation. Write the **two** words that best describe how he feels on the lines below.

pleased   excited   angry   surprised

upset   shocked   understanding   confused

Rory feels _____ but _____.

19 Based on your answer to Question 18, choose **three** sentences from the third paragraph that support your answer. Circle the **three** sentences below. Then explain what each sentence you chose shows about how he feels.

> Dad and Mom are great as always. Dad is working hard at his new job. It is going very well, and he may even have to travel to London soon. Mom is trying to get fit for our summer vacation. I know you can't make it, but you will be sorely missed. I am hoping that you will be able to make it back next year to travel with us. Any trip abroad is just not the same without you! I do understand, though. I know you are working hard and that it is all for your future.

1: _____

_____

2: _____

_____

3: _____

_____

20   Rory would be most likely to say that he is —

Ⓐ   embarrassed by Sally

Ⓑ   proud of Sally

Ⓒ   jealous of Sally

Ⓓ   confused by Sally

21   Based on the passage, what can you conclude about Rory and Sally?

Ⓐ   They are very close.

Ⓑ   They want similar careers.

Ⓒ   They are the same age.

Ⓓ   They have similar hobbies.

22   Do you think that Rory admires his sister? Use details from the passage to support your answer.

_____

_____

_____

_____

_____

23   Rory describes what each family member at home is doing. Complete the chart below by describing what each family member is doing.

Family Member	What the Family Member is Doing
Rory	
Rory's mother	
Rory's father	

24   In what way is Rory motivated by his sister? Use at least **three** details from
       the passage in your answer.

_____

_____

_____

_____

_____

_____

_____

_____

_____

_____

_____

_____

The Sahara Desert

The Sahara Desert is the world's largest subtropical desert. It covers most of North Africa. Its area is about 3.5 million square miles. This makes it almost as large as the United States of America. The Sahara Desert stretches all the way across Africa.

The Sahara Desert divides the continent of Africa into north and south. The southern border is marked by a savannah known as the Sahel. The land that lies to the south of the savannah is lush with more vegetation. The Sahara Desert features many large sand dunes. Some of these measure more than 600 feet from base to peak.

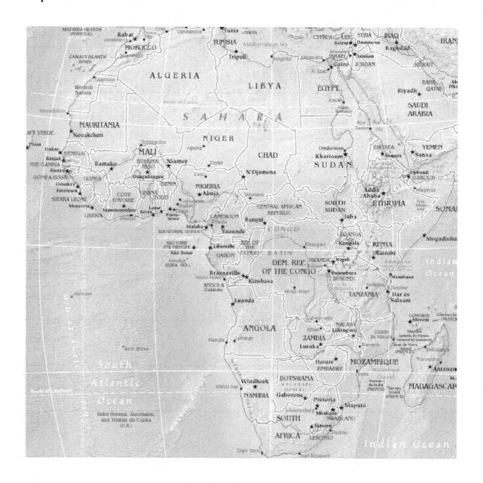

The Sahara Desert has been largely dry and with little plant life for more than 5,000 years. Before this time, it was far wetter than it is today. This allowed more plant life to thrive across its land. Thousands of ancient engravings have been found that show many types of river animals have lived in the Sahara Desert. These have been found mainly in southeast Algeria. These suggest that crocodiles lived in the region at some point in time.

The climate of the Sahara Desert has changed over several thousands of years. The area is also far smaller than it was during the last ice age. It was the end of the last ice age that brought a high level of rainfall to the Sahara. This was between 8000 and 6000 BC. Since this time, the northern part of the Sahara has gradually dried out. Though the southern Sahara still receives rain during monsoon season, it is still far less than years before. Some of the tallest mountain ranges occasionally receive snow peaks. The Tibetsi Mountains record some level of snowfall about once every seven years.

The modern era has seen several developments for the Sahara. One of these is that mines have been built to get the most from the natural resources within the region. There are also plans to build several highways across the Sahara. It is expected that one of these may be completed at some point in the future.

25 Read this sentence from the passage.

The Sahara Desert stretches all the way across Africa.

Why does the author most likely use the phrase "stretches all the way across"?

Ⓐ   To emphasize how wide the desert is

Ⓑ   To suggest that the desert is always changing

Ⓒ   To show that the desert is mainly flat

Ⓓ   To indicate that the desert has always been there

26 Read this sentence from the passage.

The land that lies to the south of the savannah is lush with more vegetation.

Explain how the word <u>lush</u> helps you imagine the savannah.

_____

_____

_____

_____

_____

_____

27   Which sentence from the passage is best supported by the map?

    Ⓐ   *The Sahara Desert is the world's largest subtropical desert.*

    Ⓑ   *The Sahara Desert stretches all the way across Africa.*

    Ⓒ   *The Sahara Desert features many large sand dunes.*

    Ⓓ   *The Sahara Desert has been largely dry and with little plant life for more than 5,000 years.*

28   According to the passage, how was the Sahara Desert different thousands of years ago?

    Ⓐ   It had fewer animals.

    Ⓑ   It was wetter.

    Ⓒ   It had smaller sand dunes.

    Ⓓ   It was home to fewer people.

29   Which of the following is most similar about the Sahara Desert and the United States?

    Ⓐ   Its size

    Ⓑ   Its climate

    Ⓒ   Its uses

    Ⓓ   Its location

30 Where would this passage most likely be found?

Ⓐ In an encyclopedia

Ⓑ In an atlas

Ⓒ In a history textbook

Ⓓ In a book of short stories

31 How is the fourth paragraph of the passage organized?

Ⓐ A problem is described and then a solution is given.

Ⓑ The cause of an event is described.

Ⓒ A claim is made and then details are given to support it.

Ⓓ A question is asked and then answered.

32 Use the map to list **four** countries that are part of the Sahara Desert.

Countries of the Sahara

33   Which sentence from the paragraph would make the best caption for the photograph?

Ⓐ   *The Sahara Desert stretches all the way across Africa.*

Ⓑ   *The Sahara Desert divides the continent of Africa into north and south.*

Ⓒ   *The Sahara Desert features many large sand dunes.*

Ⓓ   *The climate of the Sahara Desert has changed over several thousands of years.*

34   Do you think the Sahara Desert will stay the same in the future? Explain why or why not. Use details from the passage in your answer.

_____

_____

_____

_____

_____

35 Describe **three** interesting or surprising details about the Sahara Desert that are included in the passage. Explain what makes each detail interesting or surprising.

Detail	Why It's Interesting or Surprising

36   Even though life in the Sahara Desert is difficult, people do still live there. Describe **three** things that would make life in the Sahara Desert difficult. Use details from the passage in your answer.

_____

_____

_____

_____

_____

_____

_____

_____

_____

_____

_____

_____

_____

_____

The passage below contains errors. The words or phrases that are incorrect are underlined. For each word or phrase underlined, answer the question below.

Flying High

My family and I live near the airport. Some people think that's a bad thing, <u>and</u> I think it's great. I've always <u>did love</u> watching the airplanes fly way up high. They seem huge as they pass overhead. It amazes me that something so <u>enormos</u> is able to fly. Sometimes I think about who is on the plane and <u>wear</u> they are going. The planes might be mainly full of people traveling for work, but I like to imagine they are full of people on their way to explore exciting new lands.

My mom and dad <u>offen</u> complain about the noise, but not me! I love listening to the planes as I fall asleep. It makes me dream that I'm on <u>me</u> way to some exciting location. I hope that I'll always live near an airport.

37 Which of these should replace <u>and</u>?

Ⓐ but

Ⓑ for

Ⓒ or

Ⓓ then

38 Which of these should replace <u>did love</u>?

Ⓐ love

Ⓑ loved

Ⓒ have love

Ⓓ have loved

39   Which of these should replace <u>enormos</u>?

Ⓐ   enormoas

Ⓑ   enormios

Ⓒ   enormous

Ⓓ   enormus

40   Which of these should replace <u>wear</u>?

Ⓐ   were

Ⓑ   we're

Ⓒ   where

Ⓓ   ware

41   What is the correct way to spell <u>offen</u>? Write your answer below.

_____

42   Which of these should replace <u>me</u>?

Ⓐ   mine

Ⓑ   my

Ⓒ   our

Ⓓ   your

END OF SESSION 1

Florida Standards Assessment

English Language Arts

Practice Test 3

Session 2

Instructions

Read each passage and answer the questions that follow it.

For each multiple-choice question, fill in the circle for the correct answer. For other types of questions, follow the instructions given. Some of the questions require a written answer. Write your answer on the lines provided.

Beneath the Silver Stars

It was fair to say that Lucas was sometimes mean to his younger sister. He would often play practical jokes on her. His parents used to tell him that it wasn't nice to scare her. He would always say that he never meant to upset her and that he was just joking. The situation was worse when the family went camping together. Lucas would play all sorts of tricks on his sister once the sun had gone down. On one particular trip, his sister Molly was having breakfast and talking about her brother to their dad.

"Why won't he just stop playing his silly pranks?" Molly complained.

"He's just a boy," her father replied. "Although, we could get him back if you want to."

Molly raised her eyebrows. Then a smile came to her face.

"How do you mean, Dad?" she asked.

"Well, I think we should play some tricks of our own," he replied. "After all, it's just a little harmless fun. We should wait until tonight and play a few little games."

Molly was very excited at her father's suggestion and thought it was a great idea.

"We won't scare him too much will we?" she asked.

"Not at all," replied her father. "When I was a child my brother used to play tricks on me all the time. It is just something that people do, darling."

By 10 o'clock that evening, it was very dark. All of the family had gone to bed. Molly's mother was fast asleep and her father was awake but quiet in his tent. At about 11 o'clock he began to hear noises from outside of the tent. He undid the zip and peered out into the darkness. He could see Lucas making howling noises from just outside Molly's tent. He chuckled softly to himself and crept slowly out onto the grass. As Lucas continued to howl, his father made his way across and hid behind a nearby tree. Lucas then paused and began to edge closer to Molly's tent. As he did so his father let out a high-pitched howl at the very top of his voice.

Lucas stood completely still. He half turned but did not want to see what was behind him. His knees started shaking a little. His father began to creep up behind him. By now Molly was peeking out of a small gap in her tent. Lucas stared ahead of him and thought about running back to his tent. As he was about to do so, his father reached out and touched his shoulder.

Lucas leapt from the spot and ran towards his tent. Molly laughed loudly as Lucas raced away.

"You see," Molly's father said with a chuckle. "Now wasn't that fun?"

43 If the passage was given another title, which title would best fit?

   Ⓐ   Family Fights

   Ⓑ   Payback Time

   Ⓒ   How to Camp

   Ⓓ   Good Times

44 Explain why you chose the title in Question 43. In your answer, describe how the title you chose tells what the passage is about.

_____

_____

_____

_____

_____

_____

45 When the father suggests getting Lucas back, the author states that Molly "raised her eyebrows." The author describes this to show that Molly is –

   Ⓐ   confused

   Ⓑ   frightened

   Ⓒ   interested

   Ⓓ   amused

46 Circle the **two** words from the passage that have about the same meaning.

fair	pranks	harmless
chuckled	mean	peeking
tricks	scare	running

47 Why does Lucas most likely make howling noises outside Molly's tent?

Ⓐ   He is trying to scare Molly.

Ⓑ   He wants Molly to come outside.

Ⓒ   He knows that Molly is going to play a trick on him.

Ⓓ   He is trying to keep animals away from the area.

48 How is the passage mainly organized?

Ⓐ   Two events are compared and contrasted.

Ⓑ   Events are described in the order they occur.

Ⓒ   Facts are given to support an argument.

Ⓓ   A question is asked and then answered.

49   Which sentence from the passage best shows that Molly cares about her brother?

   Ⓐ   *"Why won't he just stop playing his silly pranks?" Molly complained.*

   Ⓑ   *Molly was very excited at her father's suggestion and thought it was a great idea.*

   Ⓒ   *"We won't scare him too much will we?" she asked.*

   Ⓓ   *Molly laughed loudly as Lucas raced away.*

50   Complete the web below by adding **three** more details that show that Lucas was scared when he heard his father's high-pitched howl.

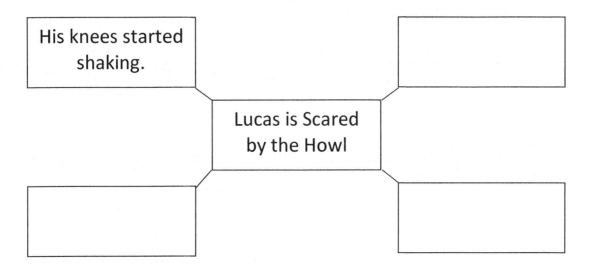

51   Which of these best explains the humor in the story?

   Ⓐ   Molly is tired of her brother playing tricks on her.

   Ⓑ   Molly and her family are trying to have a fun camping trip.

   Ⓒ   Lucas does not really want to upset his sister.

   Ⓓ   Lucas is scared by his father while he is trying to scare his sister.

52   Give **two** reasons that Molly decided to play a trick on Lucas.

       1: _____

       _____

       2: _____

       _____

53   Do you think Molly's trick will stop Lucas from playing tricks in the future? Explain why or why not.

_____

_____

_____

_____

_____

_____

Happy Campers Summer Retreat

As a parent, your child's happiness is the most important thing to you. It is important to keep children healthy and active. This can be difficult to achieve. After all, many people have busy careers as well. The Happy Campers Summer Retreat was developed to help parents with this challenge.

Michael Gibson founded our group in 1998. We run a summer camp for children during the holidays. We are open from May to September. We look after hundreds of children every single year. Our staff are all experienced and fully-trained. The camp is based in the Colorado Mountains. It offers a wide range of activities for children. Our group's mission is to create a new generation of active children across America.

Our program helps children in a number of ways. It will help develop all of the qualities listed below.

- Physical fitness
- Problem-solving skills
- Social skills
- Sports ability and experience

The Happy Campers Summer Retreat can benefit all children. Some children are good at school, but rarely active. Our program will help encourage an interest in sports. Other children are mainly interested in sports. These children will play sports, but will also learn new skills. Team sports are also very important. They are used to help children develop teamwork skills, social skills, and communication skills. Children will also have the chance to try new activities. Our program is designed to help develop a complete and fully active child.

Our program is very affordable. It is available to any family in America. Your child's stay can be as short as a week or as long as six weeks. We will also cater to any special needs that your child may have.

Why not call us today or send us an email with your enquiry? Take action now and give your child this great opportunity! Our helpful staff will be able to give you all of the answers that you need.

54 In the sentence below, what does the word <u>affordable</u> refer to?

Our program is very affordable.

Ⓐ How easy the program is

Ⓑ How much the program costs

Ⓒ How the program benefits children

Ⓓ How active children need to be

55 According to the passage, where is the summer retreat held?

Ⓐ Lake Michigan

Ⓑ Colorado Mountains

Ⓒ Yosemite National Park

Ⓓ Venice Beach

56 Which word best describes how the author of the passage sounds?

Ⓐ Serious and determined

Ⓑ Concerned and fearful

Ⓒ Positive and encouraging

Ⓓ Lighthearted and funny

57 Who is the passage mainly written to appeal to?

Ⓐ   Parents

Ⓑ   Teachers

Ⓒ   Students

Ⓓ   Sports people

58 Think about your answer to Question 57. Choose **two** paragraphs that best support your answer. Circle the paragraphs below. Then explain how each paragraph supports your answer.

Paragraph: 1   2   3   4   5   6

First paragraph selected:

_____

_____

Second paragraph selected:

_____

_____

59 Look at the web below.

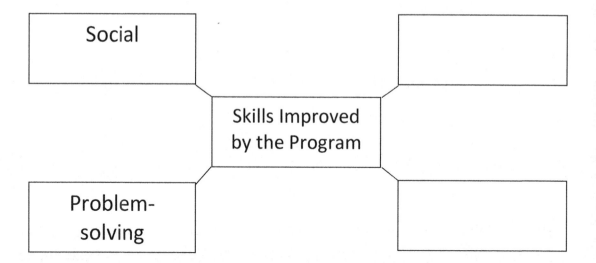

Which of these best completes the web? Write the **two** best answers in the web.

Creative thinking	Communication

Teamwork	Time management

60 The passage was probably written mainly to –

Ⓐ   encourage parents to send their children to the camp

Ⓑ   compare the camp with other activities

Ⓒ   describe the history of the camp

Ⓓ   inform parents about the benefits of outdoor activities

61   Which sentence is included mainly to persuade the reader?

    Ⓐ   *After all, many people have busy careers as well.*

    Ⓑ   *We run a summer camp for children during the holidays.*

    Ⓒ   *It is available to any family in America.*

    Ⓓ   *Take action now and give your child this great opportunity!*

62   Choose the **two** sentences from the second paragraph that best support the idea that parents can trust the camp. Tick **two** boxes below to show your choices.

    ☐   *Michael Gibson founded our group in 1998.*

    ☐   *We run a summer camp for children during the holidays.*

    ☐   *We are open from May to September.*

    ☐   *We look after hundreds of children every single year.*

    ☐   *Our staff are all experienced and fully-trained.*

    ☐   *The camp is based in the Colorado Mountains.*

    ☐   *It offers a wide range of activities for children.*

    ☐   *Our group's mission is to create a new generation of active children across America.*

The passage below contains errors. The words or phrases that are incorrect are underlined. For each word or phrase underlined, answer the question below.

Finland

Finland is a country at the top of Europe. The total area of Finland is over 130,000 Square Miles. This makes Finland the eighth large country in Europe. Its neighbors are Sweden Norway and Russia.

The capital of Finland is Helsinki. Helsinki is home to neerly 540,000 people. Finland's population as a whole is just over 5 million.

The official languages of Finland are Finnish and Swedish. Around 90 percent of the people speak Finnish. Over half of all the people also speak English good. This occurs because students in Finland has to study English as one of their school subjects.

63 What is the correct way to capitalize Square Miles? Write your answer below.

_____

64 Which of these should replace large?

Ⓐ larger

Ⓑ largely

Ⓒ largest

Ⓓ largeness

65   Which of these has the correct punctuation?

   Ⓐ   Its neighbors are Sweden Norway, and Russia.

   Ⓑ   Its neighbors are Sweden, Norway, and Russia.

   Ⓒ   Its neighbors, are Sweden Norway, and Russia.

   Ⓓ   Its neighbors are, Sweden, Norway, and Russia.

66   Which of these should replace <u>neerly</u>?

   Ⓐ   nerely

   Ⓑ   nearly

   Ⓒ   neirly

   Ⓓ   nierly

67   Which of these should replace <u>good</u>?

   Ⓐ   nice

   Ⓑ   right

   Ⓒ   well

   Ⓓ   able

68   Which of these should replace <u>has to</u>?

   Ⓐ   have to

   Ⓑ   having to

   Ⓒ   would have to

   Ⓓ   will have to

The questions below are answered after listening to a passage. Ask someone to read you the passage "Bread and Milk" from the back of this book. Then answer the questions below.

Questions for "Bread and Milk"

69   What is Niral's main problem in the passage?

Ⓐ   She does not have enough money for the bread and milk.

Ⓑ   She has to go to the store to buy bread and milk.

Ⓒ   The shopkeeper lets her buy bread and milk for five dollars.

Ⓓ   The shop is too far from her home.

70   Which word best describes the shopkeeper?

Ⓐ   Smart

Ⓑ   Rude

Ⓒ   Kind

Ⓓ   Funny

71   How does Niral most likely feel when the shopkeeper says she can have both items for five dollars?

Ⓐ   Greedy

Ⓑ   Shocked

Ⓒ   Puzzled

Ⓓ   Thankful

The questions below are answered after listening to a passage. Ask someone to read you the passage "Poor Pluto" from the back of this book. Then answer the questions below.

Questions for "Poor Pluto"

72 What does the title of the passage suggest about Pluto?

Ⓐ   It is sad that Pluto is no longer a planet.

Ⓑ   Pluto is a cold and icy planet.

Ⓒ   Pluto is too far away to be visited.

Ⓓ   Pluto's name should be changed.

73 Why was Pluto changed to a dwarf planet?

Ⓐ   It is too far away.

Ⓑ   It is too cold.

Ⓒ   It is too small.

Ⓓ   It is too rocky.

74 What is the main purpose of the passage?

Ⓐ   To instruct

Ⓑ   To entertain

Ⓒ   To persuade

Ⓓ   To inform

END OF SESSION 2

Florida Standards Assessment

English Language Arts

Practice Writing Component

Opinion Piece

Instructions

Read the passages that follow.

Then read the writing prompt and complete the writing task.

Source 1: Sleep Well, Live Well
by Anderson Lucas

I have noticed that many students are coming to school tired. I am worried about this because I think it will affect their happiness and learning. Many students have so much to do that they stay up late. It gives them time to fit in schoolwork, sports, hobbies, and time with friends. But if you do not get enough sleep, you might not do any of these things well.

When you sleep, you are preparing your brain for the next day. If you get enough sleep, you will be able to concentrate at school better and easily remember information. Studies have shown that a good night's sleep improves learning and creativity.

You need a good night's sleep for play as well. Whether you are playing an instrument or playing sport, you need to be well rested. If you don't get a good night's sleep, then you will not have the energy to fully participate. Also, your decision making and problem solving skills could suffer.

Sleep is also important for your emotional health. If you have a good night's sleep, it will be easier to control your emotions. You are more likely to feel happy and enjoy the day. If you are happy, you get along with everybody. You will feel motivated to be a good person and helps others.

Sleep is also important for your health and safety. Sleep allows your body to heal and can reduce the risk of certain diseases. If you are sick, sleep helps you to recover more quickly. It helps keep everything in your body in perfect balance. Also, if you sleep well you will be alert and react faster. This will help to prevent poor decisions. Poor decisions can put you and others at risk.

I have noticed that many students are not getting enough sleep. Please try to turn off the television, put down your phone, and go to bed earlier. If you get more sleep, you will learn better, play better, feel happier, and protect yourself and others. These are good reasons to get more sleep.

Source 2: Kids Want to Sleep In
by Noelle Zhang

I think that we should start school later in the day. My school starts at 8 o'clock in the morning, but I am very tired at this time. My mother wakes me up for school just past 6 o'clock, which is far too early. I hate getting out of bed so early in the morning. My two sisters don't like getting up either, and I'm sure there are many students who feel the same way.

I often try to go to bed at an earlier time, but I can't sleep. Sometimes I read my book with my flashlight at night. My mother tells me to turn off the light because I will be tired, but I want to stay awake and read. By the time I finally feel ready to sleep, it is very late. In the morning, I wake up feeling like I need a few more hours. I sleep in as long as I can, and then I rush to school. I often skip breakfast because I am in such a rush.

I often don't pay attention during the first class of the day because I am tired and hungry. I cannot think during class because I have not eaten breakfast. If school started later, there would be time for breakfast in the morning. There might even be time for some morning exercise. Then I would arrive at school feeling fresh and ready to learn.

I would be a lot happier if I started school two hours later. I think it would be better for everyone. I learned in science class that sleep is very important for the body. I learned that kids actually sleep more hours than adults. This is because kids are learning and growing. Students who get more sleep will be better learners. This will make the teachers happy because they will no longer be frustrated by tired students who are not listening.

I think everyone can agree that this is a good idea. Students can sleep more and can have time to eat breakfast. We can be more focused during class. Starting school later will be of great benefit to students, teachers, and parents.

Source 3: Sleep Poster
by Archer Lewis

Writing Prompt

Write an article for the school newspaper in which you argue that even though students today are very busy, they need to make time for a proper night's sleep. Use information from the passages in your article.

Manage your time carefully so that you can

- read the passages;
- plan your response;
- write your response; and
- revise and edit your response.

Be sure to include

- an introduction;
- support for your opinion using information from the passages; and
- a conclusion that is related to your opinion.

Your response should be in the form of a multiparagraph essay. Write your response in the space provided.

END OF PRACTICE SET

Florida Standards Assessment

English Language Arts

Practice Writing Component

Informative/Explanatory Essay

Instructions

Read the passages that follow.

Then read the writing prompt and complete the writing task.

Source 1: Mother Teresa
by Leonie Graham

Mother Teresa was a well-loved humanitarian of the 20th century. She was born in Albania on August 25, 1910. She died on September 5, 1997. Mother Teresa served the poor in India and in other countries. She is honored by many people and the Catholic Church for her service to the poor. She received the Nobel Peace Prize for her work in 1979 and became a saint in 2016.

Mother Teresa was born with the name Agnes Bojaxhiu. When she was a child, her mother taught her to always feed the poor. She went to an elementary school run by nuns. Mother Teresa went on a pilgrimage when she was 12. She wanted to become a nun. At 18, she joined the Sisters of Loreto in Dublin, Ireland. Later, she went with the sisters to India. She worked at a high school for poor girls in India. She taught history and geography. She also learned Hindi and Bengali in India. She made final vows to the Sisters of Loreto in 1937. She changed her name to Mother Teresa when she made final vows. In 1946, she wanted to leave the nuns to work with the poor every day. In 1948, the Pope gave her permission to leave the sisters.

She was determined to give poor people the opportunity to learn. She believed that this was the way for people to overcome poverty. She went to live in the poorest areas of India where she believed that people needed her the most. First, she opened an open-air school for poor students. When people saw the work that she was doing, they helped her. People gave money and time to help her. Mother Teresa opened an orphanage, a nursing home, and many clinics in India. She got many people to volunteer with her.

In 1971, she went to America. She opened a home for poor people in America. She also went to Beirut and Armenia to help people. She won many awards for the good things she did. Mother Teresa is thought of by many people as the greatest saint of all time.

Source 2: Jane Goodall – An Expert on Chimpanzees
by Damon Ryan

For over 50 years, Dr. Jane Goodall has studied animals and their environment. As a little girl, she observed native birds and animals. She loved to draw them and to make notes about what they did. She dreamed of traveling to Africa to see wild animals.

When she was 26, her wish came true. She traveled to Africa. She visited the countries of Kenya and Tanzania. She went to a national park in Tanzania for many years. She spent her time there studying chimpanzees. Chimpanzees are smaller monkeys covered with long black hair. They have a thick body with long arms, short legs, and no tail.

Every day she would go and observe the chimpanzees in their feeding area. She would always go at the same time. She would climb trees, copy their behavior, and eat the foods that they ate. After about two years, a chimpanzee came up to her. He did not show any fear. She named him David Greybeard. Soon he was taking bananas out of her hand. He even let her groom him. Other chimpanzees watched Dr. Goodall and David. This allowed Goodall to observe the monkeys closely.

She observed how they acted in families and how they got along with each other in the chimpanzee community. She was able to keep records on 50 different chimpanzees. That is about half of the chimpanzees in the park.

She learned many things. First, she learned that they made about 20 different sounds to communicate. They hoot, scream, and grunt. They drum on tree trunks with their hands. Each sound means something else. This is like our language where our tone of voice is used to communicate what we want to say. Each chimpanzee has a different hoot from the others. They also use their faces and bodies to communicate.

 She also saw that chimpanzees could make and use tools. For example, they would stick blades of grass and leaves into termite hills to try to get some of them to crawl out. This was the first time in history that animals other than humans were seen making tools.

In addition, she observed that chimpanzees shared emotions. They could comfort one another by hugging. They would touch each other often. They would kiss when they met. They held hands and groomed each other. She enjoyed watching the families. She was amazed that the mothers nursed and cared for their babies for five years before giving birth again.

Goodall thought all of these findings were very interesting. She found out that chimpanzees were very smart. In many ways, they were like human beings. She returned to England to study animal behavior at college.

After she finished school, it was time to return to Tanzania. She discovered more and more interesting things about chimpanzees. She gave names to each of the chimpanzees that she studied. In her journals, she recorded their behaviors and personalities. Before this time, scientists did not really know that much about these animals.

Goodall has written more than 20 books about chimpanzees. She has made 18 films about her work with them. She started the Jane Goodall Institute in Connecticut to help with wildlife research, education, and conservation. She started a program for children, too. It is called Roots & Shoots. Its goal is to help young people make a difference for people, animals, and the environment.

Goodall has been given many awards and honors for her work. She travels around the world to talk to people about protecting the environment.

Source 3: Elizabeth Blackwell – First Woman U.S. Doctor
by Carmen Santos

"It is not easy to be a pioneer — but oh, it is exciting! I would not trade one moment, even the worst moment, for all the riches in the world." –Elizabeth Blackwell

What did Elizabeth Blackwell mean when she said these words? Why did she think she was a pioneer? What could be so exciting?

Early Years of Her Life

Elizabeth Blackwell was born in England on February 3, 1821. She had four brothers and four sisters. When Elizabeth was eleven years old, her father decided to move the family to America. The voyage took seven weeks. The family lived in New York and New Jersey.

Idea of Becoming a Doctor

One of Elizabeth's friends was very sick. She told Elizabeth that she really wished there were women doctors. She thought women doctors would be kind and caring. That was when Elizabeth decided that she should be a doctor to help women like her friend.

However, medical school cost a lot. It would be about $3,000. She saved up all of her money from teaching.

Studying Medicine

Elizabeth tried to get into a college to study. Many colleges did not accept her because she was a woman. A woman had not studied medicine before.

She had to apply to 30 colleges until a college in New York finally accepted her. She began her new life as a student at the age of 26.

First Work as a Doctor

Elizabeth worked in London, England, and France and got lots of experience. Later, she returned to New York City. When no hospital would hire a woman, she opened up her own doctor's office.

One of her sisters became a doctor, too. Together they worked at a clinic for needy women and children. When they got enough money, they built a hospital. People began to respect Elizabeth. They saw the good work her hospital did. The hospital also helped train many nurses.

Elizabeth then opened up a medical school for women in New York. Fifteen students were in the first class. There were nine teachers. The school would expand and teach more students each year.

Later Years of Her Life

Elizabeth returned to England and set up another clinic. Her sister stayed in New York to run the medical school. Elizabeth was an instructor at the London School of Medicine for Women. She really loved teaching others about medicine. She liked helping women follow their dreams of becoming doctors.

Elizabeth wrote several books. One book described her work as a doctor. It was titled *Pioneer Work in Opening the Medical Field to Women*. She wrote about herself in this autobiography.

Elizabeth Blackwell, a True Pioneer

Elizabeth Blackwell was indeed a pioneer, someone who opens up and explores a new area. For Elizabeth, that area was medicine. She studied medicine when many people felt women should not. Because of her work, more and more women became doctors.

Writing Prompt

Write an informative essay about how many people who have achieved great things have followed their passions. Use information from the passages in your essay.

Manage your time carefully so that you can

- read the passages;
- plan your response;
- write your response; and
- revise and edit your response.

Be sure to include

- an introduction;
- information from the passages as support; and
- a conclusion that is related to the information presented.

Your response should be in the form of a multiparagraph essay. Write your response in the space provided.

END OF PRACTICE SET

ANSWER KEY

Language Arts Florida Standards (LAFS)

In 2014, the state of Florida adopted the Language Arts Florida Standards (LAFS). These standards describe what students are expected to know. Student learning throughout the year is based on these standards, and all the questions on the Florida Standards Assessments (FSA) cover these standards. All the exercises and questions in this book cover the Language Arts Florida Standards.

Just like on the real test, the majority of the questions cover reading standards. However, language and speaking and listening standards are also covered. The editing tasks on each practice test cover language standards, and the listening tasks cover speaking and listening standards. The answer key that follows lists the main standard assessed by each question.

Scoring Open Response Questions

This practice test book includes open response questions, where students provide a written answer to a question. The answer key gives guidance on how to score these questions. Use the criteria listed as a guide to scoring these questions, and as a guide for giving the student advice on how to improve an answer.

Scoring Writing Tasks

The practice writing components require students to write an opinion piece and an informative/explanatory essay. Use the writing rubrics at the end of the answer key to score these questions.

Practice Test 1, Session 1

Question	Answer	Language Arts Florida Standard
1	C	Determine the meaning of general academic and domain-specific words or phrases in a text relevant to a grade 4 topic or subject area.
2	B	Determine the meaning of general academic and domain-specific words or phrases in a text relevant to a grade 4 topic or subject area.
3	Step 3, Step 6	Explain events, procedures, ideas, or concepts in a historical, scientific, or technical text, including what happened and why, based on specific information in the text.
4	See Below	Explain how an author uses reasons and evidence to support particular points in a text.
5	1st, 2nd, 5th	Refer to details and examples in a text when explaining what the text says explicitly and when drawing inferences from the text.
6	A	Determine the main idea of a text and explain how it is supported by key details; summarize the text.
7	C	Describe the overall structure (e.g., chronology, comparison, cause/effect, problem/solution) of events, ideas, concepts, or information in a text or part of a text.
8	See Below	Refer to details and examples in a text when explaining what the text says explicitly and when drawing inferences from the text.
9	C	Interpret information presented visually, orally, or quantitatively and explain how the information contributes to an understanding of the text in which it appears.
10	B	Explain events, procedures, ideas, or concepts in a historical, scientific, or technical text, including what happened and why, based on specific information in the text.
11	See Below	Refer to details and examples in a text when explaining what the text says explicitly and when drawing inferences from the text.
12	See Below	Explain events, procedures, ideas, or concepts in a historical, scientific, or technical text, including what happened and why, based on specific information in the text.
13	C	Determine the meaning of words and phrases as they are used in a text, including those that allude to significant characters found in mythology (e.g., Herculean).
14	B	Determine the meaning of words and phrases as they are used in a text, including those that allude to significant characters found in mythology (e.g., Herculean).
15	See Below	Refer to details and examples in a text when explaining what the text says explicitly and when drawing inferences from the text.
16	C	Refer to details and examples in a text when explaining what the text says explicitly and when drawing inferences from the text.
17	A	Determine the meaning of words and phrases as they are used in a text, including those that allude to significant characters found in mythology (e.g., Herculean).
18	C	Explain major differences between poems, drama, and prose, and refer to the structural elements of poems and drama when writing or speaking about a text.
19	A	Explain major differences between poems, drama, and prose, and refer to the structural elements of poems and drama when writing or speaking about a text.
20	C	Determine a theme of a story, drama, or poem from details in the text; summarize the text.
21	C	Refer to details and examples in a text when explaining what the text says explicitly and when drawing inferences from the text.
22	See Below	Refer to details and examples in a text when explaining what the text says explicitly and when drawing inferences from the text.
23	See Below	Make connections between the text of a story or drama and a visual or oral presentation of the text, identifying where each version reflects specific descriptions and directions in the text.
24	See Below	Determine a theme of a story, drama, or poem from details in the text; summarize the text.

25	B	Determine the meaning of general academic and domain-specific words or phrases in a text relevant to a grade 4 topic or subject area.
26	D	Refer to details and examples in a text when explaining what the text says explicitly and when drawing inferences from the text.
27	D	Compare and contrast a firsthand and secondhand account of the same event or topic; describe the differences in focus and the information provided.
28	C	Interpret information presented visually, orally, or quantitatively and explain how the information contributes to an understanding of the text in which it appears.
29	See Below	Refer to details and examples in a text when explaining what the text says explicitly and when drawing inferences from the text.
30	See Below	Determine the meaning of general academic and domain-specific words or phrases in a text relevant to a grade 4 topic or subject area.
31	B	Determine the main idea of a text and explain how it is supported by key details; summarize the text.
32	C	Determine the meaning of general academic and domain-specific words or phrases in a text relevant to a grade 4 topic or subject area.
33	See Below	Explain events, procedures, ideas, or concepts in a historical, scientific, or technical text, including what happened and why, based on specific information in the text.
34	See Below	Describe the overall structure (e.g., chronology, comparison, cause/effect, problem/solution) of events, ideas, concepts, or information in a text or part of a text.
35	See Below	Interpret information presented visually, orally, or quantitatively and explain how the information contributes to an understanding of the text in which it appears.
36	See Below	Explain how an author uses reasons and evidence to support particular points in a text.
37	B	Demonstrate command of the conventions of standard English grammar and usage when writing or speaking.
38	A	Demonstrate command of the conventions of standard English capitalization, punctuation, and spelling when writing.
39	C	Demonstrate command of the conventions of standard English grammar and usage when writing or speaking.
40	B	Demonstrate command of the conventions of standard English grammar and usage when writing or speaking.
41	A	Demonstrate command of the conventions of standard English capitalization, punctuation, and spelling when writing.
42	one	Demonstrate command of the conventions of standard English capitalization, punctuation, and spelling when writing.

Q4.
Give a score of 0, 1, or 2 based on how many correct reasons are given.
- Possible reasons include that there may be knots and tangles, that you may hurt the dog if you comb too fast, that you may scare the dog if you comb too fast, or that you need to remove knots, tangles, or matted hair gently.

Q8.
Give a score of 0, 1, or 2 based on how well the answer meets the criteria listed below.
- It should provide a reasonable explanation of why the dog should be clean.
- It should include two problems that may occur if the dog is not clean.
- The answer may refer to the dog being hard to comb if it is dirty, to the dirt causing knots or tangles, or to the dirt causing the fur to pull. The student may also infer that the process would not remove dirt.

Q11.
Give a score of 0, 1, 2, or 3 based on how many plausible reasons are listed.
- Any reason that is based on information in the passage can be accepted.
- Possible answers could include that you have to comb the dog slowly, that there are many steps, that you comb the dog twice, that you brush the dog carefully, or that you have to condition the coat twice.

Q12.
Give a score of 0, 1, 2, or 3 based on how well the answer meets the criteria listed below.
- It should state whether the student would groom the dog themselves or pay a professional to do it.
- It should provide a fully-supported explanation of why the student made that decision.

Q15.
Give a score of 0, 1, or 2 based on how many correct lines are given. The correct lines are listed below.
- And turn your sadness into joy, / Make a smile from a frown. / And lifts you up when you are down. / To bring enjoyment out of sorrow,

Q22.
Give a score of 0, 1, or 2 based on how well the answer meets the criteria listed below.
- It should provide a clear and accurate explanation of what the statement means.
- The explanation should be related to how happiness can keep people feeling good during difficult times.

Q23.
Give a score of 0, 1, or 2 based on how well the answer meets the criteria listed below.
- It should provide an analysis of how the photograph relates to the theme or the tone of the poem.
- The answer may refer to the image as helping to create a positive or uplifting tone, or may refer to the field of flowers as something simple and natural that suggests happiness.

Q24.
Give a score of 0, 1, 2, or 3 based on how well the answer meets the criteria listed below.
- It should summarize the main theme of the poem and explain what the poem teaches about happiness and sadness.
- It should include three reasons that it is important to keep smiling or to keep being happy. Possible reasons include that it can make you feel better during sad times, that you can share happiness with others, that it makes life more enjoyable, or that it helps you make the most of every day.

Q29.
Give a score of 0.5 for each correct term circled. The correct terms are listed below.
- home plate, diamond, innings, strike zone

Q30.
Give a score of 0, 1, or 2 based on how many correct definitions are given.
- It should give a reasonable definition of any two of the correct terms for Question 29.

Q33.
Give a score of 0, 1, 2, or 3 based on how many correct roles are listed.
- Correct answers include whether players on the batting team are out, whether pitchers throw the ball correctly, whether pitchers have one foot on the pitcher's mound, and whether the ball passes through the strike zone.

Q34.
Give a score of 0, 1, or 2 based on how well the answer meets the criteria listed below.
- It should identify that the information in paragraph 5 describes the history of the game.
- It should compare this to the rest of the passage, which mainly teaches about the rules of baseball.

Q35.
Give a score of 0, 1, or 2 based on how well the answer meets the criteria listed below.
- It should provide an analysis of how the photograph helps show why an umpire is placed at each base.
- It should relate to how the photograph helps show that it could be difficult to determine whether the runner is safe.

Q36.
Give a score of 0, 1, 2, or 3 based on how well the answer meets the criteria listed below.
- It should state whether or not the student agrees that baseball is a great sport for young kids.
- It should include a fully-supported explanation of why the student agrees or disagrees.

Practice Test 1, Session 2

Question	Answer	Language Arts Florida Standard
43	D	Determine the meaning of general academic and domain-specific words or phrases in a text relevant to a grade 4 topic or subject area.
44	again	Determine the meaning of general academic and domain-specific words or phrases in a text relevant to a grade 4 topic or subject area.
45	A	Refer to details and examples in a text when explaining what the text says explicitly and when drawing inferences from the text.
46	A	Compare and contrast a firsthand and secondhand account of the same event or topic; describe the differences in focus and the information provided.
47	B	Determine the main idea of a text and explain how it is supported by key details; summarize the text.
48	3rd, 4th, & 6th	Compare and contrast a firsthand and secondhand account of the same event or topic; describe the differences in focus and the information provided.
49	A	Explain how an author uses reasons and evidence to support particular points in a text.
50	B	Describe the overall structure (e.g., chronology, comparison, cause/effect, problem/solution) of events, ideas, concepts, or information in a text or part of a text.
51	See Below	Explain events, procedures, ideas, or concepts in a historical, scientific, or technical text, including what happened and why, based on specific information in the text.
52	C	Determine the meaning of words and phrases as they are used in a text, including those that allude to significant characters found in mythology (e.g., Herculean).
53	A	Make connections between the text of a story or drama and a visual or oral presentation of the text, identifying where each version reflects specific descriptions and directions in the text.
54	3, 2, 1, 4	Describe in depth a character, setting, or event in a story or drama, drawing on specific details in the text (e.g., a character's thoughts, words, or actions).
55	B	Determine the meaning of words and phrases as they are used in a text, including those that allude to significant characters found in mythology (e.g., Herculean).
56	gulped gripped trembling	Refer to details and examples in a text when explaining what the text says explicitly and when drawing inferences from the text.
57	See Below	Describe in depth a character, setting, or event in a story or drama, drawing on specific details in the text (e.g., a character's thoughts, words, or actions).
58	B	Refer to details and examples in a text when explaining what the text says explicitly and when drawing inferences from the text.
59	D	Determine the meaning of words and phrases as they are used in a text, including those that allude to significant characters found in mythology (e.g., Herculean).
60	See Below	Describe in depth a character, setting, or event in a story or drama, drawing on specific details in the text (e.g., a character's thoughts, words, or actions).
61	See Below	Explain major differences between poems, drama, and prose, and refer to the structural elements of poems and drama when writing or speaking about a text.
62	See Below	Describe in depth a character, setting, or event in a story or drama, drawing on specific details in the text (e.g., a character's thoughts, words, or actions).
63	See Below	Refer to details and examples in a text when explaining what the text says explicitly and when drawing inferences from the text.
64	B	Demonstrate command of the conventions of standard English capitalization, punctuation, and spelling when writing.
65	B	Demonstrate command of the conventions of standard English grammar and usage when writing or speaking.
66	C	Demonstrate command of the conventions of standard English grammar and usage when writing or speaking.

67	there	Demonstrate command of the conventions of standard English capitalization, punctuation, and spelling when writing.
68	C	Demonstrate command of the conventions of standard English grammar and usage when writing or speaking.
69	whole	Demonstrate command of the conventions of standard English capitalization, punctuation, and spelling when writing.
70	C	Paraphrase portions of a text read aloud or information presented in diverse media and formats, including visually, quantitatively, and orally.
71	C	Paraphrase portions of a text read aloud or information presented in diverse media and formats, including visually, quantitatively, and orally.
72	A	Paraphrase portions of a text read aloud or information presented in diverse media and formats, including visually, quantitatively, and orally.
73	C	Paraphrase portions of a text read aloud or information presented in diverse media and formats, including visually, quantitatively, and orally.
74	C	Identify the reasons and evidence a speaker provides to support particular points.
75	B	Paraphrase portions of a text read aloud or information presented in diverse media and formats, including visually, quantitatively, and orally.

Q51.
Give a score of 0, 1, 2, or 3 based on how many correct actions are listed.
- The actions listed should be that he was stripped of his title, that he was arrested, and that he had his boxing license taken away.

Q57.
Give a score of 0, 1, or 2 based on how well the answer meets the criteria listed below.
- It should describe how Steven suggests the trick, hides in the closet, and then leaps out.
- It should describe how Jason pretends to sleep and then suggests checking the closet.

Q60.
Give a score of 0, 1, or 2 based on how well the answer meets the criteria listed below.
- It should give a reasonable explanation of why Jason has to stop himself from smiling.
- It should show an understanding that Jason knows what the noise is and knows what is about to happen.

Q61.
Give a score of 0.5 for each sentence circled that helps create suspense. Give a score of 0, 1, or 2 for the explanation.
- The student should explain why the two sentences were chosen and describe how they help create suspense.

Q62.
Give a score of 0, 1, or 2 based on how well the answer meets the criteria listed below.
- It should state an opinion of whether the trick was mean or funny.
- It should use relevant details from the passage to support the opinion.

Q63.
Give a score of 0, 1, or 2 based on how many reasonable details are given to support the idea that Marvin found the trick either mean or funny. The student may circle either sentence, and will be scored on how the sentence chosen is supported.
- To support the idea that the trick was mean, the student may describe how Marvin is scared by the trick, how he shrieks and falls backwards, how Steven and Jason laugh at him, or how he sleeps with the lamp on.
- To support the idea that the trick was funny, the student may describe how Marvin laughs about the trick, how he tries to be annoyed but can't, how he doesn't seem mad about it, or how he says "nice one guys."

Practice Test 2, Session 1

Question	Answer	Language Arts Florida Standard
1	B	Determine the meaning of words and phrases as they are used in a text, including those that allude to significant characters found in mythology (e.g., Herculean).
2	B	Describe in depth a character, setting, or event in a story or drama, drawing on specific details in the text (e.g., a character's thoughts, words, or actions).
3	A	Explain major differences between poems, drama, and prose, and refer to the structural elements of poems and drama when writing or speaking about a text.
4	5th	Determine the meaning of words and phrases as they are used in a text, including those that allude to significant characters found in mythology (e.g., Herculean).
5	See Below	Make connections between the text of a story or drama and a visual or oral presentation of the text, identifying where each version reflects specific descriptions and directions in the text.
6	C	Explain major differences between poems, drama, and prose, and refer to the structural elements of poems and drama when writing or speaking about a text.
7	C	Describe in depth a character, setting, or event in a story or drama, drawing on specific details in the text (e.g., a character's thoughts, words, or actions).
8	C	Determine the meaning of words and phrases as they are used in a text, including those that allude to significant characters found in mythology (e.g., Herculean).
9	B	Refer to details and examples in a text when explaining what the text says explicitly and when drawing inferences from the text.
10	B	Make connections between the text of a story or drama and a visual or oral presentation of the text, identifying where each version reflects specific descriptions and directions in the text.
11	6	Explain major differences between poems, drama, and prose, and refer to the structural elements of poems and drama when writing or speaking about a text.
12	B	Describe in depth a character, setting, or event in a story or drama, drawing on specific details in the text (e.g., a character's thoughts, words, or actions).
13	See Below	Refer to details and examples in a text when explaining what the text says explicitly and when drawing inferences from the text.
14	C	Determine the meaning of words and phrases as they are used in a text, including those that allude to significant characters found in mythology (e.g., Herculean).
15	B	Determine the meaning of words and phrases as they are used in a text, including those that allude to significant characters found in mythology (e.g., Herculean).
16	C	Refer to details and examples in a text when explaining what the text says explicitly and when drawing inferences from the text.
17	See Below	Describe in depth a character, setting, or event in a story or drama, drawing on specific details in the text (e.g., a character's thoughts, words, or actions).
18	C	Refer to details and examples in a text when explaining what the text says explicitly and when drawing inferences from the text.
19	B	Determine a theme of a story, drama, or poem from details in the text; summarize the text.
20	A	Determine a theme of a story, drama, or poem from details in the text; summarize the text.
21	See Below	Describe in depth a character, setting, or event in a story or drama, drawing on specific details in the text (e.g., a character's thoughts, words, or actions).
22	See Below	Describe in depth a character, setting, or event in a story or drama, drawing on specific details in the text (e.g., a character's thoughts, words, or actions).
23	See Below	Determine the meaning of words and phrases as they are used in a text, including those that allude to significant characters found in mythology (e.g., Herculean).
24	See Below	Refer to details and examples in a text when explaining what the text says explicitly and when drawing inferences from the text.

25	C	Determine the meaning of general academic and domain-specific words or phrases in a text relevant to a grade 4 topic or subject area.
26	A	Determine the meaning of general academic and domain-specific words or phrases in a text relevant to a grade 4 topic or subject area.
27	A	Describe the overall structure (e.g., chronology, comparison, cause/effect, problem/solution) of events, ideas, concepts, or information in a text or part of a text.
28	See Below	Explain how an author uses reasons and evidence to support particular points in a text.
29	See Below	Refer to details and examples in a text when explaining what the text says explicitly and when drawing inferences from the text.
30	D	Interpret information presented visually, orally, or quantitatively and explain how the information contributes to an understanding of the text in which it appears.
31	C	Determine the main idea of a text and explain how it is supported by key details; summarize the text.
32	D	Refer to details and examples in a text when explaining what the text says explicitly and when drawing inferences from the text.
33	See Below	Determine the main idea of a text and explain how it is supported by key details; summarize the text.
34	See Below	Compare and contrast a firsthand and secondhand account of the same event or topic; describe the differences in focus and the information provided.
35	A	Demonstrate command of the conventions of standard English grammar and usage when writing or speaking.
36	broken	Demonstrate command of the conventions of standard English grammar and usage when writing or speaking.
37	C	Demonstrate command of the conventions of standard English capitalization, punctuation, and spelling when writing.
38	C	Demonstrate command of the conventions of standard English grammar and usage when writing or speaking.
39	A	Demonstrate command of the conventions of standard English grammar and usage when writing or speaking.
40	B	Demonstrate command of the conventions of standard English capitalization, punctuation, and spelling when writing.

Q5.
Give a score of 0, 1, or 2 based on how well the answer meets the criteria listed below.
- It should give a reasonable explanation of the meaning of the simile.
- It should refer to how the simile compares the lion's mane to sunshine, which helps you imagine it being bright, radiant, or beautiful.

Q13.
Give a score of 0.5 for each correct word or phrase added to the table. Possible answers are listed below.
- Words to Show the Lion is Feared: fearful roar, scared all, run and hide, pray for their tomorrow, lair, truly frightening place.
- Words to Show the Lion is Harmless: roar became a whisper, soft sound, kindly home, hold his loved ones, met no harm, harmony, shared, tamed within an instant, gentle hand of love, calm forever.

Q17.
Give a score of 0, 1, or 2 based on how many relevant details are given.
- Any detail from the passage that shows Simon's kindness can be accepted.
- The student may describe how he thanks his mother for the games, how he does not argue with Thomas, how he tries to say that Thomas can play his games, or how he quickly agrees to share the games.

Q21.
Give a score of 0, 1, or 2 based on how well the answer meets the criteria listed below.
- The student should circle one of the words and provide an explanation to support the choice.
- Either answer is acceptable as long as the student explains it and supports it with relevant details.

Q22.
Give a score of 0, 1, or 2 based on how well the answer meets the criteria listed below.
- It should give an explanation that refers to how Thomas realizes he cannot use his system without Simon's games.
- It should identify that the decision is still selfish because Thomas only shares because it benefits him.

Q23.
Give a score of 0, 1, or 2 based on how well the answer meets the criteria listed below.
- The student should show an understanding that the phrase shows Thomas's feelings or emotions.
- It should explain that the phrase "his eyes lit up" shows Thomas's interest, excitement, or happiness.

Q24.
Give a score of 0, 1, or 2 based on how well the answer meets the criteria listed below.
- The student should select and circle three words that show that Thomas feels grumpy. The possible words could include *frown, gruffly, whined, shrugged,* or *firmly.*
- It should include a reasonable explanation that relates the words to how Thomas feels.

Q28.
Give a score of 0, 1, or 2 based on how well the answer meets the criteria listed below.
- It should explain how the camp encourages children to take part in sports and other activities.
- It may refer to how there are many sports and activities on offer, how children can run around, how children can try new activities, how there are fitness classes, or how the fitness program will be enjoyable.

Q29.
Give a score of 0.5 for each correct sport listed.
- Possible answers are football, soccer, baseball, basketball, athletics, tennis, rowing, or sailing.

Q33.
Give a score of 0, 1, or 2 based on how many correct benefits are given.
- The benefits may include that children get fit, that children become healthier, that children start liking sports, that children have fun, that children start to appreciate being active, or that children develop good fitness habits.

Q34.
Give a score of 0, 1, or 2 based on how well the answer meets the criteria listed below.
- It should explain that the information is biased toward making the camp sound good.
- The answer should show an understanding that the information is an advertisement or brochure, and is designed to make people want to attend the camp.

Practice Test 2, Session 2

Question	Answer	Language Arts Florida Standard
41	C	Determine the meaning of general academic and domain-specific words or phrases in a text relevant to a grade 4 topic or subject area.
42	B	Determine the meaning of general academic and domain-specific words or phrases in a text relevant to a grade 4 topic or subject area.
43	1860	Refer to details and examples in a text when explaining what the text says explicitly and when drawing inferences from the text.
44	C	Determine the main idea of a text and explain how it is supported by key details; summarize the text.
45	D	Compare and contrast a firsthand and secondhand account of the same event or topic; describe the differences in focus and the information provided.
46	C	Refer to details and examples in a text when explaining what the text says explicitly and when drawing inferences from the text.
47	See Below	Explain events, procedures, ideas, or concepts in a historical, scientific, or technical text, including what happened and why, based on specific information in the text.
48	See Below	Determine the main idea of a text and explain how it is supported by key details; summarize the text.
49	See Below	Refer to details and examples in a text when explaining what the text says explicitly and when drawing inferences from the text.
50	C	Determine the meaning of words and phrases as they are used in a text, including those that allude to significant characters found in mythology (e.g., Herculean).
51	B	Determine the meaning of words and phrases as they are used in a text, including those that allude to significant characters found in mythology (e.g., Herculean).
52	B	Determine a theme of a story, drama, or poem from details in the text; summarize the text.
53	D	Explain major differences between poems, drama, and prose, and refer to the structural elements of poems and drama when writing or speaking about a text.
54	B	Refer to details and examples in a text when explaining what the text says explicitly and when drawing inferences from the text.
55	B	Determine a theme of a story, drama, or poem from details in the text; summarize the text.
56	old wise	Describe in depth a character, setting, or event in a story or drama, drawing on specific details in the text (e.g., a character's thoughts, words, or actions).
57	See Below	Describe in depth a character, setting, or event in a story or drama, drawing on specific details in the text (e.g., a character's thoughts, words, or actions).
58	B	Refer to details and examples in a text when explaining what the text says explicitly and when drawing inferences from the text.
59	See Below	Compare and contrast the point of view from which different stories are narrated, including the difference between first- and third-person narrations.
60	See Below	Describe in depth a character, setting, or event in a story or drama, drawing on specific details in the text (e.g., a character's thoughts, words, or actions).
61	See Below	Make connections between the text of a story or drama and a visual or oral presentation of the text, identifying where each version reflects specific descriptions and directions in the text.
62	role	Demonstrate command of the conventions of standard English capitalization, punctuation, and spelling when writing.
63	C	Demonstrate command of the conventions of standard English capitalization, punctuation, and spelling when writing.
64	C	Demonstrate command of the conventions of standard English grammar and usage when writing or speaking.

65	A	Demonstrate command of the conventions of standard English grammar and usage when writing or speaking.
66	North America	Demonstrate command of the conventions of standard English capitalization, punctuation, and spelling when writing.
67	C	Demonstrate command of the conventions of standard English grammar and usage when writing or speaking.
68	D	Identify the reasons and evidence a speaker provides to support particular points.
69	D	Paraphrase portions of a text read aloud or information presented in diverse media and formats, including visually, quantitatively, and orally.
70	A	Paraphrase portions of a text read aloud or information presented in diverse media and formats, including visually, quantitatively, and orally.
71	tin cans, paper	Identify the reasons and evidence a speaker provides to support particular points.
72	D	Paraphrase portions of a text read aloud or information presented in diverse media and formats, including visually, quantitatively, and orally.
73	A	Paraphrase portions of a text read aloud or information presented in diverse media and formats, including visually, quantitatively, and orally.

Q47.
Give a score of 0, 1, or 2 based on how many correct actions are listed.
- The actions listed could include that he gave speeches, wrote letters, led the fight against the South in the Civil War, or issued an order that ended slavery.

Q48.
Give a score of 0, 1, or 2 based on how well the answer meets the criteria listed below.
- It should provide a clear and accurate description of two of Abraham Lincoln's achievements.
- The achievements identified could be becoming president, ending the civil war, helping to unite the nation, or helping to end slavery.

Q49.
Give a score of 0, 1, or 2 based on how well the answer meets the criteria listed below.
- The student should give a reasonable explanation of how Lincoln's background affects how he or she feels about his achievements.
- The answer may refer to admiring him more, respecting him more, or being more amazed by what he was able to achieve.

Q57.
Give a score of 0, 1, or 2 based on how well the answer meets the criteria listed below.
- It should describe how Chloe removes the gray hairs because she doesn't want him to look old.
- It should describe how the mother removes the darker hairs because she wants him to look gray and wise.

Q59.
Give a score of 0, 1, or 2 based on how well the answer meets the criteria listed below.
- It should make a reasonable inference about how Arnold feels at the end of the passage based on the events.
- It may infer that Arnold is pleased that he is not stuck in the middle or happy that everyone is going to get along.

Q60.
Give a score of 1 for each cause box correctly completed.
- The box for Chloe's actions should refer to how she plucks out his gray hairs.
- The box for the mother's actions should refer to how she plucks out his darker hairs.

Q61.
Give a score of 0, 1, or 2 based on how well the answer meets the criteria listed below.
- It should explain that the art shows how Arnold changes over time or how he loses his hair.
- It should use relevant details from the passage.

Practice Test 3, Session 1

Question	Answer	Language Arts Florida Standard
1	A	Determine the meaning of general academic and domain-specific words or phrases in a text relevant to a grade 4 topic or subject area.
2	C	Interpret information presented visually, orally, or quantitatively and explain how the information contributes to an understanding of the text in which it appears.
3	See Below	Interpret information presented visually, orally, or quantitatively and explain how the information contributes to an understanding of the text in which it appears.
4	F, F, F, O, F, O, F	Compare and contrast a firsthand and secondhand account of the same event or topic; describe the differences in focus and the information provided.
5	C	Describe the overall structure (e.g., chronology, comparison, cause/effect, problem/solution) of events, ideas, concepts, or information in a text or part of a text.
6	B	Determine the main idea of a text and explain how it is supported by key details; summarize the text.
7	D	Refer to details and examples in a text when explaining what the text says explicitly and when drawing inferences from the text.
8	See Below	Refer to details and examples in a text when explaining what the text says explicitly and when drawing inferences from the text.
9	D	Compare and contrast a firsthand and secondhand account of the same event or topic; describe the differences in focus and the information provided.
10	See Below	Explain how an author uses reasons and evidence to support particular points in a text.
11	See Below	Explain events, procedures, ideas, or concepts in a historical, scientific, or technical text, including what happened and why, based on specific information in the text.
12	See Below	Determine the main idea of a text and explain how it is supported by key details; summarize the text.
13	B	Determine the meaning of words and phrases as they are used in a text, including those that allude to significant characters found in mythology (e.g., Herculean).
14	D	Determine the meaning of words and phrases as they are used in a text, including those that allude to significant characters found in mythology (e.g., Herculean).
15	A	Determine a theme of a story, drama, or poem from details in the text; summarize the text.
16	A	Determine the meaning of words and phrases as they are used in a text, including those that allude to significant characters found in mythology (e.g., Herculean).
17	A	Refer to details and examples in a text when explaining what the text says explicitly and when drawing inferences from the text.
18	upset understanding	Describe in depth a character, setting, or event in a story or drama, drawing on specific details in the text (e.g., a character's thoughts, words, or actions).
19	See Below	Describe in depth a character, setting, or event in a story or drama, drawing on specific details in the text (e.g., a character's thoughts, words, or actions).
20	B	Compare and contrast the point of view from which different stories are narrated, including the difference between first- and third-person narrations.
21	A	Refer to details and examples in a text when explaining what the text says explicitly and when drawing inferences from the text.
22	See Below	Describe in depth a character, setting, or event in a story or drama, drawing on specific details in the text (e.g., a character's thoughts, words, or actions).
23	See Below	Refer to details and examples in a text when explaining what the text says explicitly and when drawing inferences from the text.
24	See Below	Determine a theme of a story, drama, or poem from details in the text; summarize the text.
25	A	Refer to details and examples in a text when explaining what the text says explicitly and when drawing inferences from the text.

26	See Below	Determine the meaning of general academic and domain-specific words or phrases in a text relevant to a grade 4 topic or subject area.
27	B	Interpret information presented visually, orally, or quantitatively and explain how the information contributes to an understanding of the text in which it appears.
28	B	Explain events, procedures, ideas, or concepts in a historical, scientific, or technical text, including what happened and why, based on specific information in the text.
29	A	Refer to details and examples in a text when explaining what the text says explicitly and when drawing inferences from the text.
30	A	Compare and contrast a firsthand and secondhand account of the same event or topic; describe the differences in focus and the information provided.
31	C	Describe the overall structure (e.g., chronology, comparison, cause/effect, problem/solution) of events, ideas, concepts, or information in a text or part of a text.
32	See Below	Interpret information presented visually, orally, or quantitatively and explain how the information contributes to an understanding of the text in which it appears.
33	C	Interpret information presented visually, orally, or quantitatively and explain how the information contributes to an understanding of the text in which it appears.
34	See Below	Determine the main idea of a text and explain how it is supported by key details; summarize the text.
35	See Below	Explain events, procedures, ideas, or concepts in a historical, scientific, or technical text, including what happened and why, based on specific information in the text.
36	See Below	Explain how an author uses reasons and evidence to support particular points in a text.
37	A	Demonstrate command of the conventions of standard English grammar and usage when writing or speaking.
38	B	Demonstrate command of the conventions of standard English grammar and usage when writing or speaking.
39	C	Demonstrate command of the conventions of standard English capitalization, punctuation, and spelling when writing.
40	C	Demonstrate command of the conventions of standard English grammar and usage when writing or speaking.
41	often	Demonstrate command of the conventions of standard English capitalization, punctuation, and spelling when writing.
42	B	Demonstrate command of the conventions of standard English grammar and usage when writing or speaking.

Q3.
Give a score of 0, 1, or 2 based on how many examples are given of things that can be inferred from the table.
- The student may refer to how De Niro has been making movies constantly since 1973, how the number of movies is greatest in the 1990s, how he is still making movies in recent times, or how only a few of the movies are comedies.

Q8.
Give a score of 0, 1, or 2 based on how many correct supporting details are given.
- The supporting details given should be those that show either De Niro's or Scorsese's success.
- The answer may refer to their Academy Award wins, how they both received the Cecil B. DeMille Award, or how the films they worked on together won awards. The answer may also refer to details that show just De Niro's success.

Q10.
Give a score of 0, 1, or 2 based on how many correct supporting details are given.
- Possible answers include that De Niro won an Academy Award for *Mean Streets*, that De Niro won an Academy Award for *Raging Bull*, or that they worked together on several box office hits.

Q11.
Give a score of 0, 1, or 2 based on how well the answer meets the criteria listed below.
- It should analyze how the sentence helps show the significance of De Niro receiving the award.
- It should explain how it suggests that only great actors receive the award or how it shows what the award means.

Q12.
Give a score of 0, 1, 2, or 3 based on how well the answer meets the criteria listed below.
- It should provide a reasonable analysis of how the author shows Robert De Niro's success.
- The answer may refer to awards he was won, the great films he has been in, the number or range of films he has been in, or statements made such as him being "one of the finest actors of his time."

Q19.
Give a score of 1 for each correct sentence circled that includes a reasonable explanation.
- Any sentence from the fifth sentence onward can be accepted. Each explanation should describe what the sentence shows about how Rory feels and indicate that he feels either upset or understanding.

Q22.
Give a score of 0, 1, or 2 based on how well the answer meets the criteria listed below.
- It should state whether the student believes that Rory admires his sister.
- It should provide a fully-supported explanation of why the student has this opinion.

Q23.
Give a score of 0, 1, 2, or 3 based on how many rows of the table are correctly completed.
- Rory should be described as completing his exams.
- Rory's mother should be described as trying to get fit.
- Rory's father should be described as working hard at his new job.

Q24.
Give a score of 0, 1, 2, or 3 based on how well the answer meets the criteria listed below.
- It should give a reasonable example of how Rory is motivated by his sister.
- It should refer to how Rory is motivated by his sister's hard work and also hopes to attend college.
- It should use at least three details from the passage.

Q26.
Give a score of 0, 1, or 2 based on how well the answer meets the criteria listed below.
- It should explain the effect of the word *lush* and describe how it helps create an image of the desert.
- It should show an understanding of the dictionary meaning of the word, as well as the connotation.
- Students may describe how it makes the savannah seem green, thriving, fertile, or pleasant.

Q32.
Give a score of 0.5 for each correct country listed.
- Possible answers include Morocco, Tunisia, Algeria, Libya, Egypt, Mauritania, Mali, Niger, Chad, and Sudan.

Q34.
Give a score of 0, 1, or 2 based on how well the answer meets the criteria listed below.
- It should state a prediction of whether or not the Sahara Desert will stay the same in the future.
- It may include an explanation related to how the desert has changed in the past, or it may provide an explanation related to the current developments described in the last paragraph.

Q35.
Give a score of 1 for each interesting or surprising detail given that includes a reasonable explanation.
- Any reasonable details can be accepted as long as the choice is explained.
- The student could refer to how animals once lived in the desert, to how large the desert is, to how the desert has changed, to how it sometimes snows, or to how there are plans to build a road across it.

Q36.
Give a score of 0, 1, 2, or 3 based on how well the answer meets the criteria listed below.
- It should describe at least three things that would make life in the Sahara Desert difficult.
- The student may refer to the large distances, the sand dunes, the lack of roads, or the dry climate.
- It should use relevant details from the passage.

Practice Test 3, Session 2

Question	Answer	Language Arts Florida Standard
43	B	Determine a theme of a story, drama, or poem from details in the text; summarize the text.
44	See Below	Determine a theme of a story, drama, or poem from details in the text; summarize the text.
45	C	Describe in depth a character, setting, or event in a story or drama, drawing on specific details in the text (e.g., a character's thoughts, words, or actions).
46	pranks, tricks	Determine the meaning of words and phrases as they are used in a text, including those that allude to significant characters found in mythology (e.g., Herculean).
47	A	Refer to details and examples in a text when explaining what the text says explicitly and when drawing inferences from the text.
48	B	Explain major differences between poems, drama, and prose, and refer to the structural elements of poems and drama when writing or speaking about a text.
49	C	Refer to details and examples in a text when explaining what the text says explicitly and when drawing inferences from the text.
50	See Below	Describe in depth a character, setting, or event in a story or drama, drawing on specific details in the text (e.g., a character's thoughts, words, or actions).
51	D	Explain major differences between poems, drama, and prose, and refer to the structural elements of poems and drama when writing or speaking about a text.
52	See Below	Describe in depth a character, setting, or event in a story or drama, drawing on specific details in the text (e.g., a character's thoughts, words, or actions).
53	See Below	Refer to details and examples in a text when explaining what the text says explicitly and when drawing inferences from the text.
54	B	Determine the meaning of general academic and domain-specific words or phrases in a text relevant to a grade 4 topic or subject area.
55	B	Refer to details and examples in a text when explaining what the text says explicitly and when drawing inferences from the text.
56	C	Compare and contrast a firsthand and secondhand account of the same event or topic; describe the differences in focus and the information provided.
57	A	Compare and contrast a firsthand and secondhand account of the same event or topic; describe the differences in focus and the information provided.
58	See Below	Compare and contrast a firsthand and secondhand account of the same event or topic; describe the differences in focus and the information provided.
59	Communication Teamwork	Refer to details and examples in a text when explaining what the text says explicitly and when drawing inferences from the text.
60	A	Determine the main idea of a text and explain how it is supported by key details; summarize the text.
61	D	Compare and contrast a firsthand and secondhand account of the same event or topic; describe the differences in focus and the information provided.
62	4th and 5th	Explain how an author uses reasons and evidence to support particular points in a text.
63	square miles	Demonstrate command of the conventions of standard English capitalization, punctuation, and spelling when writing.
64	C	Demonstrate command of the conventions of standard English grammar and usage when writing or speaking.
65	B	Demonstrate command of the conventions of standard English capitalization, punctuation, and spelling when writing.
66	B	Demonstrate command of the conventions of standard English capitalization, punctuation, and spelling when writing.
67	C	Demonstrate command of the conventions of standard English grammar and usage when writing or speaking.

68	A	Demonstrate command of the conventions of standard English grammar and usage when writing or speaking.
69	A	Paraphrase portions of a text read aloud or information presented in diverse media and formats, including visually, quantitatively, and orally.
70	C	Paraphrase portions of a text read aloud or information presented in diverse media and formats, including visually, quantitatively, and orally.
71	D	Paraphrase portions of a text read aloud or information presented in diverse media and formats, including visually, quantitatively, and orally.
72	A	Identify the reasons and evidence a speaker provides to support particular points.
73	C	Identify the reasons and evidence a speaker provides to support particular points.
74	D	Paraphrase portions of a text read aloud or information presented in diverse media and formats, including visually, quantitatively, and orally.

Q44.
Give a score of 0, 1, or 2 based on how well the answer meets the criteria listed below.
- It should give a reasonable explanation of why the student chose the title.
- It should relate the title to the theme or the plot of the passage.

Q50.
Give a score of 0, 1, 2, or 3 based on how many correct details are listed in the diagram.
- Possible details include that he stood completely still, that he did not want to turn around, that he stared straight ahead, that he thought about running to his tent, or that he leapt when his father touched him.

Q52.
Give a score of 0, 1, or 2 based on how many plausible reasons are given.
- The reasons could include that she was tired of him playing tricks on her, that she wanted to get him back, that she hoped he would stop playing tricks, that her father suggested it, or that she thought it would be fun.

Q53.
Give a score of 0, 1, or 2 based on how well the answer meets the criteria listed below.
- It should state whether or not Lucas will stop playing tricks on Molly in the future and explain the answer.
- The student may infer that Lucas now knows what it is like to be scared and so will stop, or that he will play more tricks to get her back.

Q58.
Give a score of 1 for each paragraph selected that includes a reasonable explanation of how it shows who the main audience is.
- Any of the paragraphs could reasonably be selected, but the selections made must be explained.
- The explanation should describe who the paragraph is addressed to or who the information in the paragraph is designed to appeal to.

OPINION WRITING RUBRIC

This writing rubric is based on the Language Arts Florida Standards and describes the features that are expected in student writing. Give students a score out of 4 or 2 based on how well the answer meets the criteria listed overall. Add the scores together to give a total out of 10. Students can also be given feedback and guidance based on the criteria below.

	Score	Notes
Purpose, Focus, and Organization To receive a full score, the response will: • have an opening that introduces the topic • have a clear focus • have a strong main opinion with little or no irrelevant information • be well-organized with related information grouped together • use transitions effectively to show the relationships between ideas • have a logical progression of ideas • provide a concluding statement or section	/4	
Evidence and Elaboration To receive a full score, the response will: • develop the topic with facts, details, quotations, or examples • include relevant text-based evidence when appropriate • use language to communicate ideas effectively • use language and vocabulary suited to the audience and purpose • use varied sentence structures	/4	
Writing Conventions To receive a full score, the response will: • have few or no spelling errors • have few or no grammar errors • have few or no capitalization errors • have few or no punctuation errors	/2	
Total Score	/10	

INFORMATIVE/EXPLANATORY WRITING RUBRIC

This writing rubric is based on the Language Arts Florida Standards and describes the features that are expected in student writing. Give students a score out of 4 or 2 based on how well the answer meets the criteria listed overall. Add the scores together to give a total out of 10. Students can also be given feedback and guidance based on the criteria below.

	Score	Notes
Purpose, Focus, and Organization To receive a full score, the response will: • have an opening that introduces the topic • have a clear focus • have a strong controlling idea with little or no irrelevant information • be well-organized with related information grouped together • use transitions effectively to show the relationships between ideas • have a logical progression of ideas • provide a concluding statement or section	/4	
Evidence and Elaboration To receive a full score, the response will: • develop the topic with facts, details, quotations, or examples • include relevant text-based evidence when appropriate • use language to communicate ideas effectively • use language and vocabulary suited to the audience and purpose • use varied sentence structures	/4	
Writing Conventions To receive a full score, the response will: • have few or no spelling errors • have few or no grammar errors • have few or no capitalization errors • have few or no punctuation errors	/2	
Total Score	/10	

LISTENING PASSAGES

Listening Passages: Practice Test 1

Instructions: Read each passage. After reading the passage, have students answer the questions in the test book.

A Fresh Coat of Paint

Dad decided to paint my bedroom walls. I wanted them to be blue like the sea. Mom wanted to paint them yellow like the Sun. She said it would be brighter. I thought it would be too bright.

Dad decided that we should mix the two colors together. We took the yellow paint and the blue paint. We poured them both into a bucket. After mixing the paint, I saw a pretty green color. I am very happy with the new color. My bedroom walls look great.

A Helping Hand

Dr. Price is always trying to help different people in different parts of the world. Recently, he flew to Japan to help the local doctors and aid teams after a large earthquake shook their country. The year before, he traveled to Africa to provide healthcare to people living in poverty. Each year, he travels to schools all over America and talks to students about healthcare issues. He does all this without getting paid for it.

Dr. Price is a wealthy and successful doctor in our town, and his services are always in demand. But he never forgets how important it is to help people less fortunate. Dr. Price has always believed that many people taking small steps can make a big difference. We may not all be able to do what Dr. Price does, but we can all learn from his example and find a way to help others.

Listening Passages: Practice Test 2

Instructions: Read each passage. After reading the passage, have students answer the questions in the test book.

The Little Things

Every morning when Patrick woke up he would throw up his arms, let out a yawn, and jump out of bed.

"Up and at 'em," he'd always bellow loudly.

Patrick had his breakfast and then got dressed in his overalls. He strolled out to his garden to tend to his vibrant flowers and gourmet vegetable patch.

Every afternoon, he would bring in new flowers for his wife and some fresh vegetables for dinner. He was always thankful for the meals his wife prepared and she knew the flowers were to show her he appreciated it. She always smiled as she cooked, and Patrick was sure that was why the meals were delicious.

"It's the little things that make life great," Patrick would always say.

Recycling

Recycling is important. Recycling helps keep our planet healthy. Many different things can be recycled. These include plastic bottles, glass bottles, tin cans, and paper. They are broken down and then used to make new things. This is good because the new things take much less energy to make. It also decreases the amount of waste. It's better for old items to be used to make new things than to be stored in huge rubbish dumps!

If you want to help, make sure your household recycles as much as possible. Know all the types of things that can be recycled and be sure to sort the recycled items if you need to. You might have one bin for paper, one for plastic, and one for glass bottles.

Listening Passages: Practice Test 3

Instructions: Read each passage. After reading the passage, have students answer the questions in the test book.

Bread and Milk

Niral's mother asked her to go to the store to buy some bread and milk. She gave her five dollars. When Niral got to the store, she found that the bread and milk cost almost six dollars. She knew that she needed one more dollar. She didn't want to walk all the way home without the bread and milk. She looked so lost that the shopkeeper asked her what was wrong. She explained her problem to him.

"Don't worry," the shopkeeper said. "You can have both items for five dollars today for being such a good customer!"

Niral walked home happily. She told her mother of her adventure.

Poor Pluto

Until 2006, Pluto was the ninth planet in our Solar System. It is still there, but it was renamed. It is no longer known as a planet because Pluto was changed to a dwarf planet. This change occurred because of its size. This means that while it is not a star or moon, it is not big enough to be a planet.

Pluto is farther from the Sun than all of the other planets in the Solar System. The makes the temperature on Pluto very low. A lot is still not known about Pluto because it so far from Earth. However, more will be known when a space probe named *New Horizons* flies by in July of 2015. It's been a long wait for that information. The space probe left Earth in January, 2006.

Made in the USA
Coppell, TX
03 March 2021